GROWING DREAMS

Jim Paluch

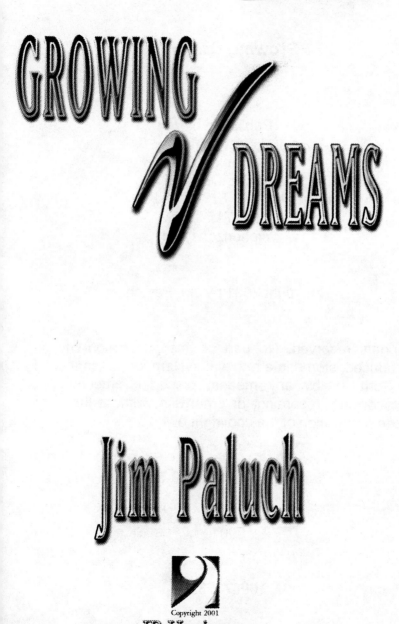

Copyright 2001

JP Horizons
INCORPORATED

Growing Dreams

Published by
JP Horizons, Inc.
P. O. Box 2039
Painesville, OH 44077
440-254-8211   877-JPH-JAMS
Fax: 800-715-TEAM
www.jphorizons.com

ISBN 0-9712815-0-5

2001

109876532

GROWING DREAMS

A Novel

Easily guiding you through the adventures of business with the ultimate goal of success

Jim Paluch

CHAPTER 1

The Beginning of a Dream

The trees, mostly oak, were losing the last of their fall splendor and the geese, forming their V against the azure sky, clamored insistently. A school bus moved slowly down the country road, air brakes first squeaking and then swooshing loudly. Red lights flashed; traffic came to a halt. The final creak assured the driver that it was safe now to release his charges into the late October afternoon.

Two boys, one nine and the other ten-and-a-half, exploded from the door as if shot from a gun, their pent-up energy erupting in jubilant screams. They bolted toward home, lunch pails and book bags swinging wildly. The brothers were on a mission, one that would last a lifetime. Reaching the end of the cul-de-sac in record time, they headed for their driveway. Curtis, the lead runner, couldn't believe his eyes: his older brother Oscar was stopping at the mailbox.

"What are you doing?" Curtis yelled in disbelief. "We gotta get the work done!" Although Oscar was exactly eighteen months to the day his senior, Curtis seemed to be the leader. His intensity and sense of urgency were always apparent in his wide-eyed gaze, fast speech, and tousled reddish-brown hair. He knew he had a customer depending on him this evening and he was not about to disappoint him. "Come on, Oscar, we got a lot of work to do before it gets dark. Come on."

Oscar, his ten-and-a-half year old frame already almost at six feet, was not phased by his younger brother's panic. Slower paced and not nearly the talker Curtis was, he knew the work would get done. "Chill out, you're gonna have a heart 'tack," Oscar shouted half in disgust, not wanting to be bossed around by his younger brother. Then he leaned over and reached into the mailbox. "I'm looking for our bank statement," he yelled. "That's what it's all about anyway, making MONEY." He tucked the mail under his arm and sped past Curtis, making sure to bump him on the way. "It's not just about money," Curtis yelled, speeding to catch up. "It's about doing a good job and keeping our customer happy. If we don't do that, we won't HAVE any money. Oscar, are you listening to me? Oscar?"

But Oscar had already leaped to the porch and hurtled through the front door. "What's all the shouting about?" his mother asked with a smile and a welcome-home hug. "It's just the slave driver trying to tell me what to do again," Oscar replied, half complaining and half teasing as he returned the hug and then hurried toward the kitchen to see what snack awaited.

"OSCAR, if we don't get the leaves cleaned up and the grass cut for Mr. Hamley's party tomorrow, he's going to be mad and we could lose a customer. The only customer we got." Curtis sped past his mother and straight into the kitchen to try to motivate the other half of his team. "Hurry up and eat 'cause we got to get to work!"

"YOUNG MAN, you'd better slow it down, or I'm going to confiscate your lawn mower." His mother's tone of voice told him that she was not kidding. "Finish up here and tell me how your day went, and then you can take care of that customer."

The boys had loaded the trailer hooked to the back of their old John Deere garden tractor and were rattling down the driveway to get to their valued customer. The rakes, tarps, brooms, and assorted other tools were neatly stacked and ready for business. Curtis was finally starting to relax a little now that they were heading to the job. Ever since the Hamleys had moved in next door and offered them the job of cutting the grass and caring for the lawn, Curtis had felt a sense of urgency about doing the work as well as he possibly could. Knowing that Mr. Hamley and his wife, both retired teachers, liked having him and his brother around left him with a good feeling, and he actually whistled as he pushed the little trim mower behind the trailer. In a minute and a half, the boys were at their work site.

"LOOK at that!" Curtis yelled to his brother over the roar of the mower. "Where did they come from?" The two boys stopped at the end of their driveway and stared in disbelief. A beautiful red truck with a black trailer full of equipment circled the cul-de-sac and came to a stop on the opposite side of the street. Following closely behind was a matching red, four-wheel-drive truck, all shiny and new. It made the same circle and parked in front of the other truck. "Cutter's Landscape Professionals," along with a fancy logo and the phone number, was painted on the side of both trucks.

The boys just stared as three men jumped out of the first truck, quickly grabbed their equipment, and almost instinctively went to work in a matter of seconds. Two more men jumped out of the second truck, one of whom fell in line with the other three. The other man, who had a tie on and seemed to be in his twenties, looked like a boss. He began to move around the cul-de-sac. At every mailbox he took a bright yellow piece of paper and rolled it to fit neatly between the mailbox and the flag on the outside. He gradually came closer to the two boys, who by now had forgotten their mission and were staring in curiosity. Rolling another flyer and sticking it on their mailbox, he walked slowly past his apparent competition. Then he stopped to look at the two boys staring at him.

"Hi, I'm Frank Cutter," he said, extending his hand. Curtis, the bolder of the two brothers, jumped forward and returned the greeting, "I'm Curtis; this is my older brother Oscar. We're landscapers." Frank Cutter just smiled and said, "Me, too." All three seemed to glance first at the equipment the brothers were using and then at the equipment being used across the street. It was a stark comparison. "Well, I got work to do," Frank Cutter said, smiling and moving toward the Hamleys' mailbox.

"Yeah, me too," Curtis responded in the deepest voice he could muster. "HEY! Don't put one on that mailbox. They're our customers!" Curtis could feel his face reddening as he moved toward his competition. "CURTIS!" Oscar yelled, trying to stop his younger brother before he did anything stupid.

"What do you think you're doing, Frank Cutter? Take that off there. Who do you think you are? I bet that isn't even your real name." Curtis was now within inches of Frank Cutter's face.

"Hey, little smart guy, they're your customers now, but they'll be mine in the spring. We're going to have every customer on this street. Welcome to the real world." Frank Cutter smiled defiantly and moved on to the next mailbox.

"Come on, Oscar, we got work to do." Curtis was nearly running with the little push mower back up the Hamleys' driveway. Both boys worked with incredible intensity throughout the evening. They put in two hard hours raking every leaf out of the yard and then giving it the best

4

cutting of the season. Curtis went up and down the sidewalk and driveway twice with the old push broom, and Oscar made sure there weren't any stray leaves back on the grass after the cutting.

Mr. Hamley had been watching them with satisfaction. "Don't you think you boys should call it an evening?" he asked with a smile as he reached for his wallet.

"We just want to make sure everything is perfect for your party tomorrow, Mr. Hamley," Curtis said, as he put his broom back into the trailer. "Did we do a good job?"

"You did a great job, so good in fact I'm going to give each of you an extra five dollars."

"THANKS!" the boys replied in unison as they received their payment and, excited, headed back down the driveway. The bonus and compliment had helped take the sting out of Frank Cutter's words. His crews were long since gone when the boys looked across the cul-de-sac to evaluate the competition's work before quickly getting everything unloaded, put away, and then hurrying to the dinner table where their favorites were waiting. Steaks and an after-dinner treat of cherry cheesecake.

"We're starting another acquisition for a client today," the boys' father told their mother as they finished up the last of the dessert. "It's going to be a big one."

"What's an acquisition, Dad?" Oscar asked. He always liked to hear about the businesses his father's CPA firm was working with and enjoyed asking questions. It seemed like the only business he knew anything about was cutting grass and, in his own words, "That is not a business."

"Well, an acquisition occurs when one company takes possession of another company. Let's say that Company A would like to work for Company B's customers. Company A could acquire Company B and make that happen. Or suppose that Company C is struggling; Company A could take possession of it and make it successful. Another kind of acquisition could occur if Company D has some technology that Company A would like to use. Sometimes, a company just wants to get bigger fast, and buying other companies is one way to do it.

My firm has to look at all the finances of the company being acquired. We look at their bank loans and statements, their sales figures, how they market their company, and how much they owe other companies, which is called "debt." Finally, we look at the people running the company and all the other employees to make sure there is a good team in place. The company doing the buying brings us a consultant to help make the final decision on acquiring the company. Does that make sense?"

"Yeah, kinda," Oscar answered, "you guys are the experts."

"Yeah, kinda." His father laughed and then looked toward Curtis, who was staring off in space. "What's on your mind tonight, young man? You're never without something to say, and you haven't said a word."

"I'm worried about Frank Cutter," Curtis blurted out." He said he was going to have Mr. Hamley as a customer next spring. He put this flyer on Mr. Hamley's mailbox and told me he was going to do all the yards on this street."

"Let me see your flyer," the father said, reaching for the yellow piece of paper. "Where did you get this one?"

"Off Mr. Hamley's mailbox. That is OUR customer and he shouldn't have put it there," Curtis replied, hoping he had done the right thing, yet knowing he hadn't.

"That was your first mistake in business," his father said. "This was not your flyer to take; it is Mr. Hamley's, and tomorrow you will take it over and give it back to him. Companies get in trouble when they try to beat their competition by using dishonesty rather than working harder and smarter. Now, as for your competition, I see he has made a mistake, too."

Both boys quickly sat up, leaned forward, and shouted, "WHAT IS IT?" Their enthusiasm made their mother and father laugh out loud.

"Well, look at this flyer," their father continued. "It says that Cutter's has the lowest prices, the newest equipment, and fancy uniforms. Big words on the kinds of things they offer, but nowhere on this flyer does it say GREAT SERVICE. That's what people really buy, GREAT SERVICE. Do you think you two offer great service?"

"Mr. Hamley gave us a five dollar tip this evening. Does that mean we gave great service?" Oscar proudly asked while showing his five-dollar bill.

"What can we do to make sure we're giving good service, Dad?" Curtis spoke with all the seriousness of one of his father's clients.

"Tell you what. I'll finish a few things in my office while you boys get your homework done, and then I'll meet you by the fireplace in the living room. We'll make a list of all the things you can do to give good service. Do we have a meeting?"

"WE HAVE A MEETING!" both boys shouted, getting up from the table and carrying their plates to the counter. "One more thing, Dad," Curtis said, "I have a name for the business, 'Growing Dreams.' Owning a big landscape business is a dream of mine because I like working with things that grow, so I just thought up GROWING DREAMS." He turned and ran out of the room before his father could comment.

Oscar was busy with a calculator as his father walked into the living room. "What are you working on, Son?"

"Our bank statement. Curtis and I were able to save $642.39 this year. I didn't think I would ever have that much money."

"That's great. How do you feel about that, Curtis?" He looked to the other half of this partnership, but there was no answer. Curtis was lying in front of the first fire of the fall, sound asleep. His father walked over and looked down at the young entrepreneur. He knew that the meeting about great customer service would have to be postponed until another day. Looking closer at his son's peaceful, sound slumber made him think that "Growing Dreams" was probably the perfect name. Curtis had made an inspired choice.

GROWING DREAMS

GROWING **P**OINT...

Remember where your dream started.

BRAIN **P**ROBE...

I wonder how many ideas I can develop and put into action that will keep the dream of my business alive and growing?

CHAPTER 2

Hard Work vs. Real Business Management

When the blasting truck horn alerted Curtis to a call on his new cell phone, he excused himself from a conversation with the homeowner he hoped would be his twelfth new customer of the week and bounded toward his '89 Dodge Ram. As he ran across the rocky clay soil of the new subdivision, he envisioned each yard green with lush sod, sod that he and his crew would lay. He leaped for the door and flew into the front seat. "Hello, Growing Dreams Landscaping, Curtis speaking." But the only response was a click. "Dang! Too late," he groaned, feeling like a fisherman who'd just lost a nibble.

At age nineteen, Curtis thought his world was a dream world. He was working ninety hours a week building his own business. His goal from the age of nine was now a dream in progress. Here he was, sitting in his new used truck with a car phone. No one else his age had a car phone, let alone their own business. He loved innovative ideas and gadgets and was having fun buying every piece of equipment he could borrow money to buy. Able to charm most prospects into buying whatever he wanted to sell them, he felt that, after his first full year out of high school, he was in much better shape than his brother Oscar, who had decided to go to college and get a business degree. "Business!" he said, thinking out loud, "I can't imagine sitting in an office every day working on some stupid paperwork." Then he remembered his potential customer and jumped down to return to the sale.

Just as the door shut, the horn blared again. This time it rang only once. "Hello, this is Curtis," he answered with an almost glad-you-called greeting. Then his tone changed abruptly as he wondered why in the world his mom would be calling at his busiest time. "Curtis, where are you? We've been waiting for you. Oscar's graduation is today, and you promised you'd go with us."

Oh no, he'd forgotten all about it, and there was no way he could make it now. "Mom, I have five more appointments before the day is out. This is Saturday, and people want to meet me on Saturday. I'll come by the house tonight for the party. I promise. Gotta go now. BYE!" As he raced back to his customer, he began calculating to see if there was any way at all he could make it to his brother's graduation party.

Oscar was standing on the front porch saying good-bye and thanks to several of his relatives as Curtis pulled up in his truck with a freshly painted "GROWING DREAMS LANDSCAPING" on the side. They watched as he finished a phone call and jumped from the truck, knocking some of the day's dust off his jeans. "Do you think he'll ever get a real job?" their old uncle whispered to Oscar as Curtis approached and greeted them. He held out his hand and gave a sincere "Congratulations" and "Sorry I missed the ceremony today." But he couldn't pass up the chance to give his older brother a hard time. "Those are pretty soft hands for a guy that used to be a landscaper," Curtis added. "But I guess guys who are planning to do nothing more than push pencils for a living don't have to be very tough."

"Hey, I can still outwork you any day of the week," his brother countered. "And I'm a lot smarter and better looking, too."

"Is there any food left in there?" Curtis asked. "I haven't eaten all day."

The guests had been gone for hours; Oscar and Curtis were sitting in the backyard discussing each other's future. "So what about it?" Curtis prodded with the same finesse he had used to close five sales earlier in the day. "Why don't you come work with me just for the summer?"

"I'm not going to spend my life pushing a lawnmower, Curtis," his brother replied. "I'm going to find a job with a company downtown, make a big salary, get a good- looking car, and belong to a country club. I'm going to use my brain and make a lot of money. That's what it's all about, man—making money."

"I'm making money AND USING MY BRAIN," Curtis said, "but it takes hard work and long hours, not just some cushy desk job."

"Curtis, how many hours did you work this week? Divide it out and you'll see you're probably making about five dollars an hour. That's not making money, that's not using your brain . . . and if you aren't making money, your company isn't making a profit. How will you pay for that truck out there and the equipment you're buying? How will you give raises to keep good people? You're not working smart; you're just working. You should consider going to college, getting a real job."

Curtis was only half listening to his brother's advice. He was thinking of the work that needed to begin on Monday and how he didn't have enough help to get it done. After a few minutes of silence, he repeated his question, trying to close this one last sale of the day. "So what about it? It'll just be for a week or two. I really need your help. You can get the office straightened around, Mr. Business Major, while you're waiting for WALL STREET to call. Come on, whaddaya say?"

Oscar laughed and shook his head, "All right, but just for a week or two, and I'm definitely not pushing a lawnmower.

"AWESOME," Curtis whooped, just as the horn in his truck started blowing again. "Hey, gotta go. My phone's ringing."

"Curtis, it's 2:00 in the morning," Oscar yelled.

"I know!" Curtis shouted back, aware that he was in the process of waking the neighbors. "It's a part time mechanic and this is the only time he can get to my place to work on equipment. Like I said, you gotta work hard. See ya 6:30 Monday morning." He headed toward the old Dodge knowing he had just closed his sixth sale.

When he drove into the parking lot at Growing Dreams Landscaping, Oscar couldn't believe his eyes. There were ten or twelve workers tripping over each other trying to get equipment both off trucks and onto trucks. Nursery stock was in total disarray; bags of fertilizer and mulch—some of them broken open—were scattered in every direction. Decks of old mowers, rusting away, were strewn about. When he pushed open the office door, it fell off its hinges. This was Oscar's first visit to the new "World Headquarters," as Curtis liked to call it, and he immediately began to wonder if he hadn't made a terrible mistake.

"YOU GOTTA DELIVER IT TODAY. I DID CALL IN THE ORDER LAST WEEK. YOU BETTER GET THE SOD CUT AND OUT THERE! I GOT GUYS LEAVING NOW, AND I PROMISED TO HAVE THIS JOB DONE TODAY." Oscar saw his brother slam the phone down and hurl his coffee cup across the disastrous office.

"Hey, you're right on time," Curtis said, this time smiling. "I thought you might wimp out, but you made it."

"What was that all about?" Oscar asked in a serious tone.

"That was just my sod supplier. I need sod for the job I sold on Friday."

"How could you have ordered the sod just last week if you sold the job on Friday?" There was silence in the room as Curtis let the question lose some of its sting. Then he darted past Oscar and headed out to conduct the morning ritual: "C'mon, let's get these crews outta here!"

Oscar watched as Curtis stomped around barking orders, quickly drawing plans and scribbling plant lists on yellow notebook paper and handing them to anyone who would take them. "You go here and pick up these plants!" he barked at a worker whose face showed that he didn't know where "here" was. "This is what the bed should look like, but don't do anything until I get there and line it out! Where's Russ? He should have been here thirty minutes ago. We need to get Barrington Ridge cut today. Hey, who ran over this wheelbarrow? That's going to cost somebody." His voice was reaching a feverish pitch as his several crews scrambled for the trucks to escape his wrath and just get on the road, ready or not. As the last of the trucks headed out the rusting front gate, Curtis turned to his brother and said, "Pretty efficient, huh? Out the gate by 7:15. Not bad."

"Curtis, those guys hate your guts. Most of them left, not caring if they do a good job today or not. I guarantee you they'll stop at the first gas station for cigarettes, take a fifteen-minute break when they get to the site, and then start lunch early and end it late. They don't care whether your shovels and rakes and other tools get damaged, and they don't care whether your trucks get dented because they'll be looking for other jobs as soon as they open the want ads tonight. That scene didn't look very efficient to me."

Curtis was boiling from his brother's know-it-all comments. If he hadn't had another sale to close and if he hadn't needed his brother so badly, he would certainly have retaliated.

"Yea, well, it's worked out so far" was all he could afford to say as he continued. "Oscar, I have a big favor to ask you. My foreman isn't here. You know Russ, the big guy who was the center for the high school football team. He misses a Monday every now and then, and I've got to get the property he was supposed to be on today cut. I know you don't want to push a mower, but could you take Julio here and go get it cut for me today? It was supposed to be done last week, and I'm dead if it doesn't get done today. Whadaya say?"

Oscar couldn't believe what he was hearing. It took everything he had in him not to walk to his car, get in, and not look back. He glanced over at his "crew" of one and then toward his nineteen-year-old brother, whose ambition was definitely bigger than his brain.

"It's against my better judgment, but, let's go, Julio."

Oscar stomped past his younger brother, headed for the truck, and then stopped, "It takes more than just hard work, Curtis. This is the last favor."

When Oscar pulled the truck up in front of the shop, all the cars in the parking lot were gone except for the one waiting for Julio. He stopped long enough for his passenger to get out. "Buenas noches, Julio. Gracias," he said tiredly as Julio smiled and shut the door. Oscar set his sights on the lone light coming from the building where he knew he'd find his brother.

Curtis heard the front door fall from its hinges and Oscar appeared instantly, standing poised for battle. The two just stared at each other. "Where ya been?" Curtis welcomed his brother with all the charm he could muster as he braced himself for the verbal onslaught that was about to erupt.

"Don't even try to sell your way out of this one, Curtis. There was no way to accomplish that job with two people in the time you said. And when I tried to call in, the radios didn't work. The mowers kept breaking down, Julio spoke no English, and every time I tried to leave, the residents came out and threatened to fire us. There were no lights on the trailer—here's a ticket to prove it—and the worst thing is, Curtis, you think you're running a good business. This place is a disaster waiting to happen, not a business!" Curtis simply stared as his brother caught his breath and continued his reprimand. "I was coming back here to tell you that I had worked my last day for Growing Dreams Landscape, but you need me." Curtis leaned forward, holding his breath for Oscar's next words.

"If you go on thinking that long hours and hard work are gonna build your business, you're crazy! It takes working smart. Here's the deal. I'm going to build this business from the inside and this is how it's going to happen. We're going to understand our customers and develop a niche. We're going to create a team of great people who like being here, and then we're going to train them with the skills needed to do the best job possible. While all of this is happening, we're going to develop systems. No more barking orders in the morning. We're going to schedule, have work orders, and create a process that takes us from sales to billing. We're also going to control costs and make sure everyone understands how to make money. And finally, we're going to share the rewards. When we make money, the team makes money."

Curtis didn't know how to respond, but somehow, deep inside, he knew his brother was right. He was only nineteen but already feeling burned out and frustrated. He was about to comment when Oscar added, "And one more thing, Curtis—integrity! This company will be run with integrity. No more lying to sod suppliers, yelling at employees, promising customers anything just to make the sale. And finally, we are going to fix that door . . . TONIGHT!"

Oscar paused, leaned forward, looked his brother in the eye, and finished his proposal. "That's the way to run a business, Curtis. It takes both working hard and working smart." Pausing again for effect, he asked his closing question. "So what's it going to be, Curtis? Are you ready to build a business?"

GROWING DREAMS

Growing Point...

It takes more than working harder; the greatest business people are always working smarter.

Brain Probe...

I wonder how many ideas I can develop and put into action that will allow everyone in the company to work smarter?

CHAPTER 3

A Company Guided by a Mission

Curtis smiled and shook his head as his older brother began to give his speech again. In the two years since Oscar had joined Growing Dreams Landscape Services, the company had more than doubled in size. They had the potential to reach one million dollars in sales and were doing it efficiently with the fourteen crew members sitting in the "pre-start jam session."

Oscar had talked Curtis into having everyone get together for fifteen minutes each morning before the crews rolled out of the gate. For a month now the attendance had been almost 100%. At first it didn't make any sense to Curtis to have fourteen people just sitting for fifteen minutes each day and getting paid for it. Now, even though he would have a hard time admitting it to his older brother, the meetings were working.

The crews were starting to know each other and develop more as a team. The customers' concerns and compliments were discussed openly in each meeting. For a month Oscar had also given them his "mission statement speech." This morning was not going to be any different.

"Let me end the meeting with the Growing Dreams mission statement," Oscar said proudly. "We commit to producing outstanding results that excite our clients, energize our team, and successfully grow our company." Oscar paused for effect, letting the words soak in before starting to ask questions. "What does producing outstanding results mean?" He had already decided that he would stand here all day until someone answered. He waited for what seemed to be forever and tried to hold back a smile. Everyone in the makeshift training room began to squirm.

Finally somebody said, "No weeds, clean uniforms, exceeding expectations, taking time to clean up at the end of the day, and making sure all of our work is quality work."

All eyes turned to the booming voice at the back of the room. "AWESOME!" yelled Curtis, getting caught up in the moment.

"Fernando, that was the best answer we ever had," Oscar added as he pulled out a new Growing Dreams hat and walked back to give it to Fernando. They shook hands and everyone applauded.

The next response came faster and the next one faster still. It was an exciting meeting that had everyone charged up. Finally Oscar asked about the last part of the mission statement. "What does it mean to successfully grow our company?"

"PROFITS," several people yelled out.

"And what do we need PROFITS for?" Oscar yelled back.

The replies came in rapid-fire succession: "better equipment" and "better facilities!" The crowd cheered when someone yelled, "Better pay!" Oscar laughed but then reiterated that profits are the only way to increase pay!

Just as he was about to wrap up the meeting one of the young foremen raised his hand and asked, "Oscar, do you have to tell us the mission statement every meeting?" A hush came over the crowd.

"HEY, JOE, you . . . ," Curtis began, but Oscar stopped him before the words he wanted to say would have put a negative cap to the meeting.

"Great question, Joe!" Oscar said with sincere enthusiasm as his bewildered brother looked on. "I am getting a little tired of talking about the mission statement. But let me tell you why I'm doing it. At a seminar in Cleveland, I heard a guy from Texas talk about the company he built, Major Landscape Services. He started with nothing and grew it to almost thirteen million dollars before selling it. He said he took every chance he had to tell the company about the mission statement. He knew they got tired of hearing it, but he never quit talking about it. A mission statement is like a compass. If a company doesn't have direction, it can't find profits and raises.

"I knew we had a mission statement. We worked on it last year, but we never used it, let alone talked about it. That's when Curtis and I talked and decided that we should talk about it in every company meeting. If it helped Major grow in Texas, it could help us here, and I've seen lots of companies trudge along and never even give thought to developing a mission statement.

"But I am getting a little tired hearing myself talk about it every morning. Joe, how about Monday morning YOU lead the conversation about the mission?"

Before Joe could object, Curtis yelled from the back of the room, "Who wants to hear Joe on Monday morning?" His question was greeted with cheers of approval and laughter. "I guess it's unanimous Joe. On Monday morning you're in charge."

As everyone stood up from the best meeting that Growing Dreams had ever had, in stumbled Russ, the company's most long-term employee. Russ ran the maintenance crews on the larger commercial properties. He knew how to get the work done but complained more than all the rest of the employees put together.

"Russ, this is the second meeting you've missed this week," Oscar said. The crews moved back as if a gunfight in an old western saloon movie were about to take place.

"I hate these stupid meetings," Russ countered. "We just go over the same stupid stuff. I'm tired of wasting my time. We should be on the site by now."

Everyone waited for Oscar or Curtis to start yelling. Instead, Russ's destructive words were met by Oscar's finesse. "I agree with you 100%, Russ; if you hate these meetings, you don't have to come."

Oscar then took his attention from the deflated Russ and spoke to the crews, "Hey, you bunch of SUPERSTARS! I know you've had enough meeting for today. Head for your trucks. Fernando, can you fill in for Russ for a little while today out at Barrington Ridge?"

"SURE, BOSS!" Fernando responded with pride at having been appointed to a supervisory position, even if it was just for a few hours. His new hat seemed to glow as he signaled his crew to follow him to the truck.

"Thanks, guys," Oscar said as Curtis handed out as many high-fives as possible. It was now just the three of them standing in the quietness of the mechanics' bay. Oscar looked up at Russ. "Do you have a minute?"

"Don't lay that Dale Carnegie stuff on me. I'm standing here, ain't I?"

"Great, why don't we just go into the office?" Curtis asked, knowing what was about to take place.

Curtis sat behind his desk. Russ plopped down in a chair and assumed the same position that he always did: arms crossed, eyes staring at the floor, and a big pouting frown on his face. Oscar leaned against the wall and let his brother begin the conversation. "Russ, you and I have been friends since elementary school, and I hope we're friends for a long time. Oscar and I have been talking and well . . . you see . . . it's . . . hard. . . ."

"Oscar, tell him about the Builders' and Destroyers' thing you were telling me about."

Oscar was prepared to help his brother. "Russ, I read an article several months ago about two types of people in a company; they were called 'Builders' and 'Destroyers.' I won't bore you with all the details . . . but Destroyers are the people that hate everyone—management, customers and co-workers. They're the ones that try to tear down everything that the company is doing. They arrive late, complain, and try to ruin everyone else's attitude. Russ, the article actually described how you act around here. That's why. . . ."

Curtis jumped in before his brother could finish. "That's why we're going to have to let you go. It's a hard thing for me to say, but I think you'll be happier someplace else. We'll give you two-weeks pay and whatever we owe you for this last pay period. But today is your last day at Growing Dreams."

"Big deal. Cutter Landscape has been begging me to work for them," the destroyer said. "You guys won't make it without me."

"Well, we're willing to try," Curtis said, moving around his desk to hand his longtime friend a check. Then he reached out to shake Russ's hand and direct him to the door.

"I'm proud of you, Curtis," Oscar said as they watched Russ walk toward his truck. "That wasn't an easy thing to do, but Growing Dreams is a better company because you did it.

"Watch how everyone steps it up. We won't even miss him. He'll help us more working for the competition than he did working here."

"You're right," Curtis said, forcing a smile. "Well, I have some sales calls to go to. No sense sitting around here and dwelling on it. Why don't you see if you can stay awake here in the office today and get something accomplished?" Oscar knew Curtis was doing what he always did when he felt a little blue; he was trying to be funny. "I'll tell you what, Oscar. If I come back here this afternoon and it looks like you got something accomplished, I know a great restaurant we can have a meeting at this evening."

"I'll look forward to that." Oscar joked back. "Will you forget your wallet again this time, or should I just plan on paying for it again?"

GROWING DREAMS

GROWING POINT...

Passionately tell the Mission Statement at every opportunity.

BRAIN PROBE...

I wonder how many ideas I can develop and put into action that will allow me to keep the Mission Statement on the hearts and minds of every person within the company?

CHAPTER 4

The Customer Service Formula

The restaurant was full as the two brothers entered and walked up to the hostess. "We have a reservation for seven o'clock," Curtis said with his usual charm. "The name is Cluznik. My first name is Curtis. What's yours?"

"Right this way Mr. Cluznik. Your table is ready." As she turned to lead the two young businessmen to their table, Curtis noticed that her rosy cheeks were turning even rosier. Pulling a chair out for Curtis and placing a leather-bound menu in his hands, she said, "Here you are. I hope you enjoy your dinner this evening. And by the way, my name is The Future Mrs. John White." It was then that Curtis noticed the spectacular diamond engagement ring she was wearing.

"Wow," Oscar laughed, "I hope you had better luck this week selling landscape services than you did trying to get a lead from that last prospect. If not, we'd better not order much from this expensive menu. When did your taste change from fast food? Did you see the prices on this stuff?"

"Forget the prices, big brother. Did you notice Mrs. John White's excellent service and communication skills?"

"Man, you are changing. That is the first time I have ever heard you mention anything about a girl's customer service or communication skills. Usually it has something to with her. . . ."

"Good evening, gentlemen." Oscar's ribbing of his brother was cut short by a well-dressed and very proper waiter standing at attention and ready to serve. "My name is John, and. . . ."

"You're not John White, are you?" Curtis asked, not quite able to get his mind off the last conversation.

"No, sir. Why do you ask?"

"No reason, just curious." Curtis said, motioning for John to continue.

"Yes, sir. I will have the privilege of serving you gentlemen this evening. It is our entire staff's commitment to ensure you have an enjoyable dining experience." The two young businessmen were mesmerized as the professional waiter explained the menu to them, detailing the chef's specials for the evening and introducing them to his assistant, who quickly returned with beverages and a loaf of warm focaccia. I will allow you to browse the menu and should you have any further questions, please ask. I will be back shortly to help you finalize your selection for the evening."

"What in the world are we doing here?" Oscar asked as he glanced down the menu. "I'm not sure I can remember everything he told us and have you actually looked at the prices?"

"Forget prices. This is a business meeting and an educational session on customer service and understanding your market niche. Welcome to an upscale market niche, Brother." Curtis set the menu down and Oscar saw that familiar idea-generating look in his eyes. "Let me tell you about my past week of sales calls, Oscar."

"Go ahead. You don't mind if I begin eating some of this bread while you're talking, do you?"

"This is my week. I had five new calls with residential clients in new homes wanting a landscape design and various degrees of installation. I also met with three past customers wanting to do the next phase of their projects. Then there were two new property managers interested in Growing Dreams doing a proposal for landscape maintenance and an architect for a new office building wanting us to bid on the landscape installation."

"Okay, that sounds like a pretty good week," Oscar said, buttering up another slice of the best bread he'd ever eaten. "What's the point?"

"That's only a portion of the appointments I handled. Let me fill you in on the rest. I had four appointments to see if we cleaned out downspouts. Three wonderful little old ladies wanted to know what the bugs on their plants were. Two people wanted someone to water the plants in their houses while they were on vacation. One man wanted us to take care of his dog, and another wanted psychological testing for dreams he was having. He thought our name, Growing Dreams, was a sleep analysis clinic. Oscar, if you total up the time for these appointments and various other phone calls that I made answering questions from people who were not even close to a client, I wasted over fourteen hours this week. What could I do with fourteen extra hours?"

"Pardon me, sir." The maitre d' and his assistant were at their table. "Are you gentlemen prepared to make a selection?" He carefully guided them through the menu, nearly applauding every choice and making them feel as if they were the only diners in the entire restaurant.

"That was quite an event," Oscar said as the waiter left their table. "I feel pretty special being here this evening. That kind of service almost makes it a pleasure to drop $150.00 on a meal."

"Oscar, look around. There are some great lessons to learn here this evening. Think about the market niche that this restaurant has created. They are in the restaurant business; that is the market they serve. Joe's Diner and McDonald's and Subway and Pizza Hut are also in the restaurant business. What is important is that each has a certain niche that they have chosen to serve. This place has created a market niche around serving people that are willing to pay $150.00 for dinner for two. It is their commitment to be the best in that niche. Their professionalism separates them from the competition and has this place full of people enjoying the experience of 'feeling special.' What is our niche, Oscar? Have you thought about it?"

"Here are your salads, gentlemen." The waiter proudly placed both plates on the table as his assistant filled the water goblets for the third time. As the waiter quickly moved away, sensing that a conversation was taking place and not wanting to disturb it, they were encouraged to "enjoy."

"WOW! This salad is a work of art," Oscar said, getting more and more used to the luxury he was partaking in for the evening. "Let's see, our market niche. Well I know we are in the landscaping business."

"Great guess," his younger brother said, trying to get him to be a little more specific. "But what is the niche?"

"Well, we seem to do a lot of residential new homes needing landscapes, but we also do some existing landscape renovation as well. Then, there is all the subdivision work we do for builders. We are doing more and more bid work for architects and developers. We have a good size mowing business for condominiums, and there are the couple of office parks we do. This year we started the irrigation crew and we are two years into the lawn-fertilizing business, not to mention pond installations and the exterior lighting work we do. With the extra land in the back, the nursery is starting to come on and there seem to be more and more people stopping in to buy retail. I almost forgot about wintertime with the Christmas tree sales and then all of the snow plowing. I guess when you think about it, we have a lot of niches."

"STOP!" Curtis said, placing his fork on the table and throwing his head back to stare at the ceiling. "STOP! You are ruining my appetite and making me tired. We do all of that and more. Oscar, that is insane. What would it be like if this wonderful restaurant also served a good, greasy hamburger or thick crust pizza along with Chinese food and donuts? What would you think of peanut shells on the floor, waiters in tuxes, and a cook in the back that fixed your transmission while you ate your meal? How about your date getting a pedicure at the table? It would be ridiculous, disorganized, and nowhere near the pleasant atmosphere they've created here, plus they would have a hard time charging the money that they do. These owners made a decision and defined the market niche they would go after; they decided they would not try to be everything to everybody. They created their market niche and worked to dominate that niche. They have it figured out; we haven't . . . YET!"

"May I take your plate, sir?" The waiter's assistant politely lifted their salad plates, readjusted the remaining silverware, scraped the crumbs from the table, filled the water glasses and disappeared.

"AMAZING," Curtis said, as he pulled a piece of paper from his daytimer. "Look at this formula I wrote out today. I called it the CUSTOMER SERVICE FORMULA. CS=AP/CE. The CS part is simple. That stands for customer service. That needs to be the end result of every company desiring to dominate their market niche. Outstanding CUSTOMER SERVICE!"

"Gentlemen, please excuse me. It is my pleasure to serve the meals that have been exquisitely prepared for you by our chef." The entrees were presented with the care of a jeweler presenting a fine diamond. "I will stop back momentarily, gentlemen, to make sure everything has been prepared to your expectations."

"Curtis, you can continue talking and I will do my best to continue listening, but my expectations are to enjoy every bite of this meal!" Oscar, in a short time, had now become a connoisseur of fine food.

"That is a great lead in to the next part of the equation. The 'CE' stands for customer expectations and that is exactly the denominator that allows our experience here to be as AWESOME as it is tonight. They understand the expectations of every person walking through their front door. They know that their market niche expects to be greeted by a pleasant, professional and poised hostess. Not to mention beautiful. What a boring name that will be for her: Mrs. John White."

"Hey, I'm doing my best to pay attention to what you're saying, but I'd like you to pay attention to what you're saying also. Now. You were talking about expectations." Oscar successfully brought Curtis back to reality.

"Right! They know their customer expects the excellent, professional attention that Ol' John is giving here along with his assistant. They know to have the lighting just right. The décor is appropriate, the silverware and tables are perfect, the presentation of the food and every mouthwatering bite are designed around the expectations of the customers they have chosen to serve."

"You are making sense, Curtis, or it just might be the food. So, you don't think we understand our customers' expectations?"

"Understand their expectations? We don't even know who our customers are, let alone understand their expectations. But I'll get to that before the night is over!"

"Gentlemen, excuse me for interrupting. Have your dinners been prepared to your satisfaction?" Once again, John and his assistant were standing at attention next to the table.

"John, I don't know when I have ever enjoyed food more." Oscar's taste had climbed to another level in the past forty-five minutes. "The food, service, atmosphere, and your attention to detail have been an incredible performance! Thank you!"

"THAT IS THE 'AP' PART OF THE EQUATION!" Curtis said, raising his voice to a level that caused the future Mrs. John White to look from the hostess stand, smile, and simply shake her head. "The AP stands for 'actual performance.' When an organization understands a customer's expectations, it can then focus on the performance that will allow the company to meet or exceed those expectations. John, do you have a minute?"

"Of course, sir. Is there something you need? Is your meal not up to your standards?"

Oscar just laughed and said, "John you are talking to an individual who lives on leftover bologna sandwiches. Your meal is meeting his standards."

"Don't listen to him, John. He's intoxicated by his experience here. I need to know, John, what the owners of this restaurant do to create the atmosphere and the incredible commitment of the employees' 'actual performance' to exceed the customers' expectations."

John seemed to welcome the question and the opportunity to answer it. "Sir, you may not remember my greeting when I first met you this evening. Your remembering it is not important; what is important is that I remember it. I greeted you with a greeting that told you our mission statement, 'It is a privilege to serve every guest through a team committed to ensuring an enjoyable evening and a remarkable dining experience.' All of us are committed to that mission statement. We hear it many times a night. It is part of our staff meetings. We constantly look for ways to make that mission statement more than just words. Next, the owners are constantly recruiting individuals that look at it as a privilege to serve people. I had sent a resume here and went through two months of interviews and testing before they hired me four years ago. I know I am lucky to be here and serving you this evening."

Curtis was writing down every word that John was saying. "Great, John. Your mission statement is the guide and you hire only the best people. What else?"

"Then, we teach, and teach, and teach. No team member will be placed in front of a customer until we are absolutely sure that he or she can deliver our mission statement in word and in performance. Then comes the most important part. We listen to our guests. Each month we invite three to five of our guests to a lunch here in the restaurant. Every team member is required to be here, from the dishwasher to the chef to hostess and waiter. We are paid to have a wonderful lunch and to listen to what the clients expect when they come to our restaurant. We list all of their expectations and the following week we have a one-hour brainstorming session on what the team members can do to exceed those expectations. Everyone gives input and no detail is left out, from lighting to the words we say. Everything is considered for improvement. From these guest meetings, we come to know exactly whom we are serving, what they like, and how we can deliver an enjoyable dining experience. You know what else?"

Curtis stopped writing and both he and Oscar leaned forward for more. "We send the guests home from those meetings with gifts and a certificate for dinner for two. Already this evening, I have had three new guests tell me that they are here because one of their friends participated in the lunch meeting and told them about our mission statement and the entire team's commitment to it. Mr. Cluznik, I think it is safe to say that we work very, very hard at ensuring our 'AP' exceeds your 'CE.' Thank you for asking. Now, I must let you finish your dinners and introduce you to the best part of the evening, the dessert tray. I hope I did not take too much of your time." John again disappeared, leaving the brothers' heads spinning with ideas.

"That is incredible!" Oscar said.

"Do you mean my CS =AP/CE formula was just illustrated with John's explanation?" Curtis asked, allowing his self-imposed genius status to become apparent.

"No!" Oscar said, holding back his smile with a serious look and setting down his fork beside a clean plate, seeing another opportunity to irritate his brother. "This food was AWESOME. The best I ever ate. I'm not very good at trigonometry formulas, so I'm still not sure what the heck you're talking about"

"DANG IT, OSCAR, I'M SERIOUS HERE!" Curtis's tone brought another glance from the hostess stand and this time a role of the eyes as well as a big laugh from his older brother.

"I am too, Curtis. Relax. Don't be so stressed; I'll cover the check here this evening. It was worth it. Here's what I learned from your formula and John's mini-seminar." Oscar handed his yellow legal pad to Curtis with the following three goals on it.

- We have defined who our customers are and what it will take to dominate this niche we have created in our market.

- We have developed a process to understand and communicate customers' expectations that is systematic and well defined.

- We have increased our commitment to using the mission statement to drive our actual performance to meet the expectations of the customers in our market niche.

"YEAHHH," said Curtis. "That is exactly what I'm talking about. So, when do you want to work on a plan to make these goals a reality?"

"How about right after dessert?" Oscar asked, motioning to John.

Getting up from the table, they once again thanked John for the sumptuous dining experience. Walking past the hostess stand, they were greeted again by the hostess that had started their evening.

"I hope you had a wonderful dining experience with us, Mr. Cluznik."

"Let's just say, The Future Mrs. John White, that your AP far exceeded my CE, ensuring your tremendous CS." Curtis's comments were met with a blush, a rather long ten seconds of silence, followed by a look that said, "You're different" and, finally, "Have a good evening, Mr. Cluznik."

"That is our first lesson, Oscar: making it a pleasure for our clients to spend money with us. Creating an event and separating ourselves from the competition."

GROWING ✓ DREAMS

GROWING POINT...

Customer service equals the company's actual performance determined by the client's expectations.

BRAIN PROBE...

I wonder how many ideas I can develop and put into action that will help us dominate our market niche through outstanding customer service?

CHAPTER 5

Qualifying the Customer

The goals that were created at dinner the night before were written big on the easel and flip chart.

- We have defined who our customers are and what it will take to dominate this niche we have created in our market.

- We have developed a process to understand and communicate customers' expectations that is systematic and well defined.

- We have increased our commitment to using the mission statement to drive our actual performance to meet the expectations of the customers in our market niche.

Each Growing Dreams team member stopped and read them prior to grabbing a piece of pizza and finding a seat in the meeting room. During the ride home after dinner last night, Curtis and Oscar had decided that there was no need to wait on moving toward accomplishing these three goals. They decided to initiate a voluntary meeting for anyone that wanted to come and had called everyone from the car that evening to tell them about it. The room had a curious buzz as Curtis walked to the front, shut off the ROCKY music, and began to speak.

"This may be the most serious and important meeting we have ever had here at Growing Dreams and I'm not surprised to see that every employee has shown up for a voluntary meeting. It is amazing what pizza will do." Everyone laughed nervously and Fernando slowly raised his hand.

"Yes, Fernando, what is it?" Curtis asked. Fernando slowly rose to his feet and cleared his throat. "Big Boss, all of us want to thank you. What you did yesterday, when you let Russ go, made us all proud of you. He was a destroyer, yes, but he was also a friend of yours. We were talking and know that was not an easy decision for you and Mr. Oscar. You have earned even more of our respect and all of the team applaud you and promise to work even harder."

Curtis and Oscar looked at each other and nodded as the applause stopped. "Thank you, Fernando, and all of you. That was not an easy decision, but great businesses are not built on just making the easy decisions. They are built on hard ones. Russ will find another job and, hopefully, help someone more than he was able to help us. But that decision is history. We have some more exciting decisions to make this evening. Let's get started. Here is our mission statement:

"We commit to producing outstanding results that excite our clients, energize our team, and successfully grow our company." Curtis, with Oscar's help, went on to tell them about the meal they had last night and what they had learned, the customer service formula, the week of appointments he had and how the three goals could literally make the difference in the future of Growing Dreams.

"The first goal is what we are here to achieve this evening," Oscar said, "and it would be impossible without your input. You are going to help us define who our customers are, and once we accomplish that, we will then be able to focus our efforts on being the number one choice for those customers. WE WILL DOMINATE THE MARKET." Curtis reached over and hit the ROCKY theme song as Oscar got on a roll. "WE WILL BE THE BEST." Everyone stood up and was giving high fives; Curtis couldn't believe the energy but knew something great was happening.

"All right!" Oscar continued. "Here is the process. What better way to identify who our customers are than to draw pictures of what they look like. We are going to break into four teams of four. Take these markers and big pieces of paper and the first warm-up exercise will be to draw a picture of what our customers aren't . . . let's call them the unqualified client."

"Hey, Oscar, what if you do not know how to draw?" one of the crew leaders asked with sincere concern. He was supported by "Yeah, and I can't even draw water from a well," which got several strange looks from the rest of the team.

"It doesn't matter," Oscar laughed. "Do the best you can with it. Each team will have a few minutes to explain their drawing. Let's get started. You have a half hour to do the drawing." With that, he once again cranked up the music and the room was buzzing with laughter and focused discussion on the "unqualified client."

As the thirty minutes came to a close, Oscar realized it was going to be like stopping a freight train. Everyone was so involved in what they were doing that it was hard to get their attention. He shut off the music and yelled, "That's it, gather around everyone. Come on you bunch of Picassos. It's time to stop."

They all began to move back to their seats, laughing and trying to get a sneak preview of the others teams' drawings. Team by team, Oscar had them come up and present their drawings and explain them. Then they hung all the pictures beside each other and Oscar flipped over a clean sheet of paper. "Okay, let's list the similarities in the drawings and then from that list we'll have the criteria of the unqualified client for Growing Dreams." People began to shout out answers and Oscar began to write.

- They like to do the work themselves.

- They want to get a lot of bids and pick the cheapest.

- They do not let their spouse in on the decision-making.

- They do not want to pay for a design or consultation.

- The house or property is not fitting of a large landscape project.

- The first thing they say is they do not have a budget for the work.

- They will buy the plants somewhere else and we will plant them.

Oscar would keep asking "What else?" to keep them adding ideas, and when he felt they had exhausted the possibilities, he concluded with, "Does this give us a good idea of who is not a Growing Dreams client?"

He was greeted by a chorus of, "It sure does," and "We always have trouble with that type of client," and Curtis added, "They are the hardest ones to sell to. From the exercise, it has convinced me that I will quit trying to sell to them."

Michelle, who had been the office manager for over a year and set the appointments when people would call in, said, "I will no longer try so hard to set a meeting with that type of client when they call in. I always assumed we wanted to meet with everyone and sell everything we could, but now I realize that is not necessary. In fact, sometimes it actually hurts the company."

Curtis and Oscar looked at each other and smiled. They knew that in order for their new focus on dominating their market niche to become a reality, they would have to get Michelle to understand it. It all began when the phone rang, and that is when the process would begin to get refocused.

"Great job, guys! Now that we know what an unqualified client looks like, how about drawing the client that is qualified to work with Growing Dreams?"

Oscar did not have to coax them into the drawing exercise this time. As soon as he had suggested it, they were back in their teams and going to work. Everyone was sharing ideas, picking up markers, laughing and learning together. At the end of thirty minutes, Oscar brought them all back together and once again the artists displayed their creations. All four drawings were hung side by side and Oscar stepped up to the easel to begin writing.

"All right, what are the similarities of these drawings, beside evidence of drug abuse amongst the team?" People started shouting ideas and Oscar began to write:

- They appreciate quality.

- They value freedom and their time.

- They drive nice cars.

- They make a lot of money.

- They can make a decision based on the best person to do the job.

- They know the value of landscaping.

- They are interesting people.

- They need landscaping to attract people to their building (if it is a commercial property).

- Price is not the first consideration.

- They usually have seen our work somewhere.

- They are very demanding but considerate.

- They have a great house.

- They keep up with the Joneses.

- They are not looking for little "grunt" labor work.

"WOW! What a list!" Curtis yelled from the back of the room. He had been trying to stay somewhat quiet in the exercise to gain an understanding of how the rest of the company was perceiving the customer. "Can we find enough customers like that?"

Everyone laughed and then Michelle, who was really participating in the exercise, ignited the room when she stood up and said, "You know, if we are not wasting our time in marketing, selling, and performing work for people who are on the unqualified list, then it will allow us more time to find, sell, and do work for the people who are qualified customers. It will make everybody's job better and the company more profitable."

"Great!" Curtis responded, "Michelle, why haven't you told us stuff like that before? You really hit the nail on the head."

"Hey, you didn't ask until now!" Curtis knew she was right. "Up to this point, I always thought you just wanted any work that called in. So, that is why I accepted any call and gave it to you as a lead or tried to set an appointment. NOW, I know differently. What I suggest we do is create a statement that describes our customer. It will be like our mission statement only give us direction on who the customer is."

"Great idea, Michelle," Curtis said. "Why don't you take that marker out of Oscar's hands and run the meeting? At least we'll know the words are spelled correctly."

"Hey, she won't have to take it," Oscar said, giving it an underhand toss. "She can have it! It's all yours, Michelle." Oscar moved to the back of the room with Curtis. Both of them were excited about a member of the team stepping forward to lead this important meeting.

Michelle stepped up, flipped over a new piece of paper, and said, "All right, let's get started. One sentence that describes the type of customer we want to work with. We will call it our MARKET STATEMENT." She wrote the words big on the top of a sheet of paper.

The next half-hour produced a variety of adjectives and descriptive phrases that continued to be honed, analyzed, and revised, creating another excellent exercise for the Growing Dreams team to be working through. When Michelle finally stepped back from rewriting the twelfth revision, the following sentence appeared on the flip chart.

"We will successfully serve the high-end residential construction or commercial-maintenance client that values landscaping as an investment."

"Does this mean no more simple sod jobs that take only two hours to do but can waste a day preparing for and then people call mad at us because the sod died and they didn't water it?" Fernando was painting a picture of the exact scenario that Curtis and Oscar wanted to move away from. "We can't make money on that can we, Big Boss?"

Curtis laughed and said, "You're absolutely right, Fernando. There is little to no money to be made on those jobs and they have the potential for lots of frustration."

Curtis looked again at the MARKET STATEMENT written on the board. Then he gazed across everyone that had just spent the last hour and a half of their own time coming up with that statement and a better understanding who the Growing Dreams customer was. Although he felt great that they had the statement, a quietness and uneasiness came across the room. He was wondering what had happened. Then it became clear when Michelle made an important statement.

"Curtis, speaking of frustrating, I'm a little frustrated. Now that we have this MARKET STATEMENT, I'm not sure what we do with it. When someone calls in do I say, "EXCUSE ME, Mrs. Prospect, but are you a high-end residential construction or commercial-maintenance client that values landscaping as an investment?" Michelle's theatrics and simulated phone conversation brought a chuckle from the crowd.

"Yeah, and do you drive a nice car and have lots money?" one of the crew members chimed in as they al continued to laugh.

Curtis understood the uneasiness. Just coming up with a statement was not enough. There must be a process behind it that everyone understands. He looked over at Oscar in a way that said, "HELP!"

"YOU'RE ON THE RIGHT TRACK!" Oscar announced with a clap of his hands. "Michelle, you're absolutely right. We just need to come up with the right questions to ask that will help us qualify that client as one that fits into our market niche. Why don't we do that before this meeting comes to an end? What are the questions we can ask at the initial phone call to determine if the client is a qualified client for Growing Dreams? Michelle, you have the marker. Why don't you keep writing?"

Curtis and Oscar could see the wheels turning in Michelle's head. This was going to be different. The process that was getting developed was going to directly affect her! It was more responsibility, and they hoped she would be able to accept it. The next move told them they were on the right track. When Michelle began to speak, they realized it was not fearing the responsibility that she was thinking about but how to make this process work.

"I think we need no more than five questions." She began with energy and confidence that had this tough crew of landscapers giving her their full attention. "And, it needs to be accomplished in less than three minutes. Any more than that and I am spending too much time on the phone and I can possibly be wasting the customer's time. So how about five good questions?"

nando yelled out, "WHAT COUNTRY CLUB DO ᠍ ᠍ᴺG TO?" Everyone laughed.

..aybe a bit more subtle than that, Fernando," Michelle said, only half laughing at his joke. For the next twenty minutes, they worked through potential questions to the amazement of Curtis and Oscar. When it was finally concluded that they had five good questions and Michelle felt she could use those questions, she stepped back and read them out loud, with commentary on why each was helpful.

QUESTION 1: What are the specifics on your home or project?

"This will give me the neighborhood they live in or the type of commercial property it is. If I know that it is the neighborhood or type of project location we want, I can continue getting more details. If not, I begin to direct them to another resource for help. We have names of several smaller companies that I will refer people to."

QUESTION 2: How did you hear about us?

"Their response to this says a lot. If they said we were going through the yellow pages looking for landscape companies, I have an idea that they are shopping for the best price or have a small project. If they say one of our clients referred them, then I can talk briefly about which client and what they like about the work we do for that client. A good client referral is the best prospect. They also may have seen our trucks in their neighborhood or attended our garden show display. These would also be good responses from a potential qualified client."

QUESTION 3: Has our reputation in this area and commitment to our clients earned us the right to be the only resource to developing or maintaining your landscape?

"WOW! That's a big, bold, brassy question," Curtis said. "I love it. It lets us know who the competition is."

"That's right, Curtis," Michelle said, her enthusiasm building, "and listen to this response I thought of for both of the potential answers from the prospect. If they say YES, meaning we are the only one they are working with, then I simply say 'GREAT! Thank you for your confidence.' Then I move to question number four!

"But, if they say 'NO, we are looking at other firms,' then I say, 'GREAT! Who else are you considering and may I suggest a few of the more qualified?' If this is done successfully, I can either find out who we are competing against or at least know we are competing against good competition."

"DON'T GIVE THEM CUTTER'S NAME!" one of the foreman yelled, "I don't want to send any business their way. I bet that's where Russ ends up working." The rest of the team agreed.

Oscar just smiled and said, "Hey, one good thing about Cutter's is they charge a high price. I would rather compete against somebody that knows their time is valuable and charges accordingly, rather than the low-baller that is just barely making a living. Still doesn't mean I like Cutter's though, Joe!"

"All right, no competition bashing now. We'll come up with a list of good companies to recommend to the qualified and the unqualified client," Curtis said, laughing at the competition aggression taking place. He thought it was a healthy thing. The team was committed to winning. "How about question four, Michelle?"

QUESTION 4: What are you considering having us help you accomplish at your home?

"This is a key indicator of the qualified client. I want to get the exact details of what they want to accomplish. If it's laying a little sod, then I recommend them to someone else. And how about this idea, Curtis?" Michelle stopped and seemed to let the idea incubate for a moment. "If they are an unqualified client and I recommend them to someone else, then I will send a short note to them on one of our Growing Dreams cards to thank them for considering us, wish them luck working with whomever they choose, and suggest they contact us if they ever consider a project we would be more efficient at helping them with."

Curtis fell off his chair for effect with a loud bang onto the floor. Everyone jumped up and looked back at him and began to laugh. "You're knocking me out, Michelle, and all of you guys, too. Imagine getting a note from a contractor that didn't do work for you. They'll tell their friends about us, even though we're not the company doing the work. I love it! Tell me about question five."

"Well," Michelle hesitated, "this may be the toughest one, but if I have developed a good relationship with the person on the phone, if I have been professional and courteous, then I have a good chance of getting question five answered."

QUESTION 5: Have you established the budget for the things you described in question 4?

"If they say 'YES,' then I say something like 'GREAT.' I thought you may have, based on our conversation. What is the range you are considering? If done correctly, I hope they will just tell me and that will help you, Curtis, when you go on a sales call."

"YOU KNOW IT!" Curtis yelled, this time standing up on his chair and letting out a loud cheer.

"And if they say 'NO,' do you know what I say?"

"GGGRREEEAAAATTTTT!" Everyone laughingly answered her in unison.

"You got it," Michelle continued. "And then I will follow it up with something like, 'With all of the criteria that goes into establishing a professional landscape, most people wouldn't have a definite idea of cost. However, what most of our clients did have was an idea of what their overall financial budget would allow them to do, at least initially. Do you have a range in mind for this project?'"

Again, from the back of the room came a loud bang and crash as Curtis once again fell from his chair. Getting back up to the laughter of the entire Growing Dreams team he yelled out, "Michelle, I LOVE YOU ! ! !" which brought even more laughter. "If you can accomplish getting the budget and the answers to all of the questions, then we have an idea at that point if this is a person we will want to work with! A QUALIFIED CLIENT THAT MEETS THE CRITERIA OF OUR MARKET STATEMENT."

"What do you mean IF!" Michelle said, her confidence continuing to grow. "This process begins today. YOU JUST BETTER BE ABLE TO SELL 'EM, AFTER I QUALIFY 'EM! And by the way, I won't mention the love comment to my husband."

"HEY, AMIGOS! LET'S GET READY TO DOMINATE THE MARKET ! ! ! ! !" Fernando yelled, standing to lead an ovation for Michelle.

"LET'S DO IT!" Oscar said. "See you all in the morning!"

Curtis and Oscar thanked Michelle for her help and as she walked out the door Oscar suggested, "Since dinner was so productive at the restaurant last night, we ought to go back tonight." But when he looked at Curtis, he knew his evening of work was just beginning.

"SHE WAS RIGHT, YOU KNOW!" Curtis was now pacing around the office. "She's going to have the prospect qualified and ready to go. I have to be able to sell them on Growing Dreams and why we are better than the competition. Come on, Oscar, we have some work to do yet this evening," he said, turning the flip chart to a clean sheet of paper. "We need to TANGIBILIZE THE INTANGIBLE!"

GROWING ✓ DREAMS

GROWING POINT...

Creatively and completely distinguish the qualified client from the unqualified client.

BRAIN PROBE...

I wonder how many ideas I can develop and put into action that will always have the company working with the most qualified clients?

CHAPTER 6

Tangibilizing the Intangible

"I think I have a bologna sandwich here in the refrigerator. Do you want a soda or something?" Curtis seemed to be just getting started at two thirty in the morning. Oscar was hanging on, trying to keep up with him and could only laugh when Curtis mentioned bologna, remembering their incredible meal only last night or the night before. Oscar couldn't remember anymore.

"No, Curtis. You go right ahead. The only thing I would like is some sleep."

"SLEEP?" his brother questioned, "How can you think about sleeping? We almost have this thing figured out. I'll be right back." Oscar leaned back in his chair and tried to get a few minutes of sleep before his brother returned. "I GOT IT, OSCAR!" Curtis said, bursting back into the office, bologna sandwich in hand.

"Got what, botulism?" Oscar answered, almost falling out of his chair. "Is the bread on that sandwich supposed to be blue?"

"I got the sale process! We will call it QUALITY PERFORMANCE SELLING . . . QPS. It will be supported by a QUALITY PERFORMANCE PLEDGE . . . THE QPP! What do you think? Huh? What do you think? Curtis took a big bite out of his sandwich and waited anxiously for an answer.

"It sounds to me like you must have found some leftover alphabet soup out there as well. It sounds A-O.K. to me, but if we don't wrap it up ASAP, PDQ, I am going to K.O. Y-O-U!"

"Would you get serious?" Curtis laid his sandwich down on the chair and moved toward the easel and paper. His brother braced himself for the journey he knew he was about to go on. When Curtis was excited, there was no stopping him or redirecting him. The best thing to do was just hold on and get excited with him as his plan unfolded.

"We have been talking about it all night, the process that I go through to sell. It is this," and he started to write:

1. We get a lead.

2. Somebody sets the appointment.

3. I go to the first appointment.

4. I come back to the office and prepare a proposal.

5. I present the proposal.

6. I hopefully sell the job.

"What is different about that process from any other company in this city?"

Oscar leaned forward, thought for a moment, and then said, "Well, I heard some people just mail their proposal to the prospect. At least you go back and present it."

"Anybody that just mails a proposal to a qualified client is missing a big opportunity, and I will outsell them every time. That is one thing different, but, for the most part, this process is the same. We need to do something different through the process. That is where the Quality Performance Pledge comes in. The QPP will be a document, Oscar, that I will present when I go back to present the proposal for the landscape. It will detail exactly how this client wants Growing Dreams to service them. We will have in writing everything that they mention they want us to do. If they want separate billings on commercial sites, it will say that in the QPP. If they want to pick out the plant material for their home, it will say that in their QPP. If they want us whistling "Born To Run" while we plant trees, it will be listed in the QPP. The Quality Performance Pledge will be our way of tangibilizing the intangible. We will separate ourselves from the competition by putting in writing everything the client is EXPECTING US TO DO!"

The two young entrepreneurs were now both talking at once as they decided to recreate the six-step process Curtis had outlined and spend the rest of the night developing the system to make the QPP a reality! They took turns writing and rewriting until the process began to take shape.

THE QUALITY PERFORMANCE SELLING PROCESS

STEP 1: Acquiring the lead.

- All leads will be entered on a lead sheet on the computer. (Michelle creates.)

- A first appointment is set immediately if called in or within 24 hours if acquired some other way.

- A card goes out to thank them for calling us and to say we are looking forward to the appointment.

STEP 2: Setting the appointment

- When calling to set an appointment with a qualified client, the QPP concept will be introduced by saying, "Mr. Prospect, when we meet I will also introduce to you the Quality Performance Pledge. This is an idea unique to Growing Dreams that helps us to make sure we perform for every client exactly the way they want us to. I look forward to getting your opinion on the QPP and putting it to work for you."

"That is a big move," Oscar said, no longer concerned with sleep and getting excited about the breakthrough idea they were working on. "In my college marketing classes, they call it USP, unique selling point. It is the finding something to separate you from the competition and then presenting it to the customer at every possible opportunity. When we tell the customer about it before even meeting with them and then tell them that we are looking forward to getting their opinion on the QPP Process, then we are already developing a relationship and separating ourselves from the competition. I LOVE IT CURTIS. What next?"

- Send a note to remind them of the appointment and to say we are looking forward to the opportunity to earn their business.

STEP 3: The first meeting.

- Ask questions and take notes, introduce the QPP and, if appropriate, give a short introduction of the company and the portfolio.

- The date for the follow-up meeting to present the QPP and proposal is set before leaving the house.

"You know something, Oscar. I remember when I first started selling. I would go into a meeting and think I had to do all the talking. I would tell them all about us. Number of trucks, people, insurance, all the stuff that they really didn't care about. Then I would go through the EVERYBODY LIST. I would tell them about the best quality, experience, twenty-four hours on call, best equipment, best, best, best, best. . . . I called it the EVERYBODY LIST because I realized it was exactly the same thing that everyone else was telling them. That's when I tried to stop talking so much and started listening. I even started taking notes, but then there was never anything to do with those notes . . . UNTIL NOW. That is the next part of the process."

STEP 4: Send a Discovery Letter.

- Within 24 hours of the meeting with a client, a letter will go out detailing the key points of the meeting and their major concerns, a brief description of how we will address those concerns, a reminder of the follow-up date, and a statement that that the entire Growing Dreams team is looking forward to earning the right to be a resource to them.

"Until our meeting with the team last night, I would have thought 'Sure, when will you get time to do this?'" Oscar said, growing more excited about the professionalism of the approach. "But with the decision to be more selective and to understand who qualifies as a Growing Dreams' client, you will not be running after everything that calls in and your time will be better spent pursuing the clients we want to work with. This is all a pretty smart move, little brother. Now if I could just get you to do something with this half-eaten sandwich sitting on the desk, I could concentrate better."

"You'll be able to concentrate, Oscar. Are you sure you don't want a bite?" Curtis taunted his brother, handing the sandwich to him and then quickly gobbling it down. "Listen, this process is just going to keep getting better. Remember my customer service formula, $CS = AP/CE$? With this process, we are beginning to understand and concentrate on the customer's expectations, the CE! We will then be able to document those expectations with the next step.

STEP 5: Prepare the Proposal.

- The proposal becomes a package consisting of the contract, the drawing (if one is needed), and the QPP.

- The QPP is prepared by taking the notes from the meeting on the specifics of the client's expectations and listing them in the QPP.

- The QPP is then discussed with the production staff to make sure the client's expectations are understood and can be met. If there is agreement between sales and production, then a "signing ceremony" takes place, getting as many team signatures as possible on the QPP.

- If there is something in the customer's expectations that the production team feels they cannot achieve, then a discussion takes place and the salesperson must address this change as well as an alternative with the client when the QPP is presented.

The brothers were excited working through step five. They realized they had systematically created a marketing tool, a quality assurance program, a tool to get production more involved in the sales process, and a process of accountability for the actual performance of the team. The customer service formula that had just seemed like a bunch of letters to Oscar the night before was now the foundation to a very exciting program they were calling Quality Performance Selling. The two most important steps of the process still needed to be written.

Curtis looked at his watch. It was four thirty in the morning. "Hey, you lightweight. Do you still have what it takes to get the rest of this written or do you need to go to bed?"

"I have what it takes, even though I know you'll take all the credit for it. I want to at least make sure it gets done correctly." Oscar gave his younger brother a high five and said, "Let's get it done."

STEP 6: Presenting the Proposal

- The QPP is presented to the prospect prior to unveiling the drawing or proposal.

- Each of the key items of the QPP is discussed with the prospect along with an overview of how this criteria will be accomplished to meet the client's expectations.

- The prospect is shown all of the team's signatures on the second page of the QPP, emphasizing that everyone at Growing Dreams is interested in doing their work.

- The prospect is asked to sign the QPP, with the understanding that the signature does not mean that they are obligated to working with Growing Dreams; it merely means that the customer's expectations have been clearly stated and understood by the company.

- When they sign it, move into the presentation of the proposal or drawing.

- If they do not sign it, the trust factor may not be there and the salesperson will decide whether to pursue presenting the proposal and drawing.

They knew the last part of that step was different and difficult. Curtis wondered if he would have enough discipline to walk away from the potential sale if the customer would not sign the QPP. If it was going to be the process and the philosophy, then the only way it would work is if he stood by it no matter what, regardless of how big the potential sale was.

STEP 7: THE SALE ! ! !

- Asking for the sale would be a natural part of the process if the previous six steps were adhered to. A relationship is developed and now the client has a clear choice of Growing Dreams as a professional and progressive company or choosing somebody else with the hopes that they could follow through on their promises.

- A sale consists of a signed QPP and a signed contract, with payment terms and a deposit check.

The seven-step Quality Performance Selling process was complete and both of the young entrepreneurs liked it. It had the potential to help in every aspect of their business that had been discussed since the dinner at the upscale restaurant. The "CS" was being addressed and determined as they had begun to define their market niche and focus. The Quality Performance Pledge was going to allow them to determine the expectations of every individual client, the CE of the formula, and be able to communicate those expectations to the individual that would provide the actual performance, the AP.

"I like what we have accomplished in the past two days, Curtis." Oscar was trying to be as serious as possible. "It's taking us to a more professional level."

Curtis did not answer right away. He was looking out the window at the Growing Dreams team members getting out of their cars and getting prepared for another day. "The team, Oscar! We need to be working on that team continually. We have to develop the culture that will bring the best people to us, those wanting to be a part of the company. Then we have to train. If we are promising all of these things through the QPP and are positioning ourselves to DOMINATE the market, we have to make sure there is a dedicated team to sustain it."

"Hey, what are you two doing in here?" Michelle's enthusiastic voice brought them back to reality. "It looks like the two of you have worked all night also. Curtis, I have a lead sheet and script that I put together last night. I couldn't sleep thinking about qualifying the customer and dominating the market. I'll leave it here on your desk next to this UGH, awful-looking sandwich. When you get time, let's go over it. Right now, Fernando has some things to discuss with the crews on improving performance to dominate the market. Everybody got pretty excited last night. And now I have just one more thing to say to you: take a shower before your first qualified appointment today!"

Curtis and Oscar just looked at each other. Growing Dreams was actually beginning to take off!

"She's right, you know. You really should shower this week." The sandwich just missed Oscar as he scooted out the door.

G<small>ROWING</small> P<small>OINT</small>...

Separate yourself from the competition by tangibilizing the intangible.

B<small>RAIN</small> P<small>ROBE</small>...

I wonder how many ideas I can develop and put into action that will separate us from the competition?

CHAPTER 7

Creating a Training Challenge

Oscar cleared his throat as he prepared to give his first speech as president of the local chapter of the state landscape association. Shifting in his seat and feeling butterflies performing an air show in his stomach, he glanced over at the nearly one hundred members finishing dinner. It was not the number of people that made him nervous, but the fact that the format of his presentation was rather unconventional. Glancing to the back of the room, he saw his younger brother Curtis giving him a big grin, the same mischievous grin that he'd been using since he was three years old, the one that signaled he was about to do something that could get him in trouble. Oscar knew they were both on the brink of doing just that.

He snapped back to reality as the association's state executive director announced his name. Jumping to his feet and moving to the podium, he shook the director's hand and looked out over the half-interested crowd. After some scattered applause, there was a deafening silence. "Thanks for coming tonight," he began. "I know that what I have to say ranks third here this evening, right behind the steak and beer." A few chuckles and a lot of clapping relayed the crowd's agreement.

Oscar hesitated and checked to see that Curtis was in position by the closed double doors at the back of the room. Then at a volume that blew members back in their chairs, Oscar yelled, "THAT'S WHY WE'RE GOING TO DO SOMETHING DIFFERENT HERE TONIGHT!" As the words echoed, Curtis flung open the doors. In marched the local high-school band blasting the "Rocky" theme song. As the landscapers looked on in total surprise, the team from Growing

Dreams Landscaping came running in with cheerleaders throwing confetti and shooting silly string. The crowd gave a rousing standing ovation.

"Now that I have your attention," Oscar continued as everyone sat back down, "let me tell you what I want to accomplish in my presidency. TRAINING. TRAINING. TRAINING. I know we need it at every level of our companies. I know we want to do it. But how are we going to do it? How do we find time and how do we keep it going fifty-two weeks a year? Here is my training challenge to you. I challenge every company in this room to a contest to see who can train for fifty-two straight weeks starting right now. Curtis!" Oscar looked to his brother in the back of the room.

"Yes, Mr. President!" his brother replied, snapping to attention and waving the Growing Dreams crew in. Immediately they taped up twelve big sheets of paper, each labeled with a month. Curtis continued, "Now, I'd like to ask all of you to take the sticky notes placed at your table and write down all of the training topics you would like to cover in a year, one per sticky. Then post them on the most appropriate month. After that, we'll break into groups. Each group will decide the seven or eight most important topics to train on for their month. When we're done, we'll have a fifty-two-week training calendar, along with some alternative training topics. Any questions?"

From the back of the room came a stirring of chairs. It was none other than Frank Cutter and his twelve people, including Russ, an ex-Growing Dreams employee, getting out of their chairs and heading for the door. "Where are you going?" Oscar yelled. "I don't want to play any stupid games and my guys are already trained. You're wasting our time with this idea and just showing off. I don't have time for this!" Everyone just watched as the twelve dissenters made their exit.

"Well, anybody else not have time for training?" Oscar asked, looking back at Curtis giving him a thumbs up. "Now's the time to leave," he said boldly, all the while praying they'd stay. No one else left. Crisis successfully avoided. "Let me tell you the rest of the game. After we establish our calendar, there will be a price for any company wanting to participate. Each company must prepare at least one topic outline and a facilitator's guide for that topic. A few may need to do two.

"These outlines are due at the chapter office in five days." That comment was met with some grumbling. "Now come on," Oscar continued, "that is a small price to pay for a fifty-two-week training program. It just needs to be a simple outline that everyone can follow, and each individual company will be responsible for adding the real hard facts to the outline."

Oscar could tell everyone was interested but knew he'd better wrap it up. "Here's the challenge," he continued. "Every Tuesday at 7:00 a.m. every company in this room will be training on the same subject, at the same time, for a half hour with all employees. You know what that will make each of us do? Stick with it. If I know my competition is training, I'll be training. If we're all doing this, each company will be better and this association will be doing just what an association should be doing for its members."

The members sat in silence. They were unaccustomed to dealing with innovative ideas at an association meeting, especially on steak and beer night. Oscar looked toward Curtis, who was motioning from the back of the room to ask for questions. Curtis knew from his sales experience that it was good to get the prospect talking. "Uh, any questions?" Oscar asked in anticipation.

Several hands went up and one well-fed individual in the front row stood and said, "I train with videos. My crews sit in front of a video every Tuesday morning at 6:00 a.m. Why would I need to do this?" He sat back down, thinking he had training under control within his company until his well-meaning foreman added, "You mean they SLEEP in front of a video every Tuesday morning." The crowd chuckled.

"Videos are great—as part of a program," Oscar said, "but videos can't do everything. I read in *PRO* magazine that training needs to be participatory. It needs to teach people how to think, not just memorize facts and information. I want us all to find a way to get people to participate. I think this process will do it."

"I don't want to have to prepare and teach a training session every week," someone else responded. "That's the beauty of this training challenge," Oscar replied with enthusiasm. "Let your staff teach it. For example, who should train on the weeks that deal with mechanical issues?"

"The mechanic," the group responded.

"And on office procedures?"

"The office manager!" they agreed.

"Bed edging?" Oscar continued.

"The foreman!" they yelled back.

"See what I mean?" Oscar continued. "Getting the staff to teach and train benefits both the trainer and the rest of the team."

"I let the foreman do the training on site." A contractor with a booming voice stood to make his comment and presence known. "I expect them to do the training. It's part of their job."

"You're absolutely right!" Curtis replied in the same booming voice, unable to hold back any longer. "But how do we know they're training on the right things? If we can give them a foundation to build on with these weekly training sessions, they will be that much more effective with their training in the field. "Besides," Curtis strategically added, "I know we are the only company that can win this challenge. We'll have no problem training for fifty-two weeks straight."

Curtis's comment hit its mark. The rest of the companies in the room either mumbled, shouted, or cheered that they would be the company to train for fifty-two weeks. The intensity level and volume of sound in the room grew until Oscar had to bang on the microphone to get everyone's attention.

"Hey, Oscar!" thundered the voice in the back of the room. "If your brother there thinks your company can win, why don't he put his money where his mouth is?"

"Why don't we all?" replied Oscar. "How about this? For the company that trains for fifty-two straight weeks, everybody else will come and do a spring clean-up at their office and cook the entire company a barbecue with all the trimmings."

"Where do we start?" someone ready to take the challenge shouted.

"We need a fifty-two-week calendar," Oscar answered. "Pick up the pens and sticky pads, write your training needs down, and stick them on the wall. LET'S GET STARTED!" Oscar motioned to the band director, who instantly blasted out another tune for the thinking, hustling, writing crowd that had begun to roam the room.

"Wow! That was a long meeting," Curtis said as he and his brother carried the stack of flip-chart sheets through the parking lot. "But it was the best one this association has ever had. This is really going to benefit everyone."

"YOU'VE GOTTA BE KIDDING ME!" yelled Curtis as he stopped in his tracks and looked at his truck's slashed tires. "Who do you think did that?" he growled at his brother, "and why are you smiling?" Oscar couldn't help but smile. "You know who did it: Cutter or one of his guys. And I'm smiling because we have our competition right where we want them. They're afraid of us, Curtis. They know that doing this training along with everyone else in the area is going to make us all better. The big guy in town is about to lose his big advantage. Yes sir, they're afraid. They know consistent training is going to make a difference. Yep, we have 'em right where we want 'em."

GROWING DREAMS

GROWING POINT...

Training creates the future.. . .

BRAIN PROBE...

I wonder how many ideas I can develop and put into action that will consistently introduce technical and personal skills in such a way that teaches everyone to think?

CHAPTER 8

Scoreboards Track Company Results

Curtis walked into the foremen's area and began to survey the five scoreboards placed around the room. It had been forty-two weeks since they'd begun the Training Challenge and all of the twenty-two companies that had started the program had kept their vow to train a half hour each week. He was amazed how it had drawn the landscape association together and boosted the level of professionalism across the board. At the last meeting, a member had come up to Curtis, excitedly shaking his hand and saying, "This Training Challenge has transformed my company. Everyone, from the office to the installation and maintenance crews, now appreciates the skills required and the challenges others in the company face."

Curtis was excited about what it was doing for the association and even more stirred up about what it was doing for the company. The scoreboards were evidence that training was making a difference at Growing Dreams. Before the first training session, Curtis and Oscar sat the entire company down. They discussed the training schedule planned for the coming year and asked, "What measurements can we use to make sure the time spent training is making a difference here?"

After an hour of great discussion, they came up with five measurements that Oscar put into charts on five poster boards, which were placed in the foremen's office with the training bulletin board in the center. Both Curtis and Oscar felt the presentation of the scoreboards and the bulletin board made a great statement of their commitment to the Training Challenge.

Now, months later, the scoreboards clearly showed improvements taking place. Curtis smiled every time he looked at them. The first was titled "Out the Gate by 7:00 a.m." Since the group had decided everyone would gain from training on loading and organization techniques along with teamwork and efficiency awareness, they assigned and scheduled training on these issues. A different crew each week monitored progress. They would get loaded and ready fifteen minutes early and then wait at the gate, checking off each crew that made it out before 7:00 a.m. and cheering as they left.

The chart showed the results for each week. Curtis was gratified to see they had a four-week string of 100% out the gate by 7:00 a.m. A year ago, it would have been cause for celebration if anyone got out on time. This one measurement alone had created incredible camaraderie and commitment to improvement.

The next scoreboard showed customer compliments, not complaints. The whole idea was to build up teams and motivate them by positive strokes. They had developed a survey to leave with each client at project completion. At the end of each week, the number of forms returned with high marks from the client would be posted on the chart.

At first they were getting only 10-15% back. But once the foremen saw the compliments customers submitted, they became motivated for more. They pushed to ensure quality work and began actively promoting the surveys to customers. The company now receives 75% of surveys back and is shooting for a goal of 100%. As the salesperson, Curtis was also excited at how many referrals he was getting on the forms returned.

Curtis never thought employees would propose the third scoreboard, the one to measure productivity, but bringing employees into the planning process had given them a greater feeling of ownership than he had guessed. They had risen to the occasion. To establish standards on how to measure productivity, Curtis and Oscar called contractors around the country that they had met at ALCA events. In the process they learned how to budget hours for each job. The productivity scoreboard was simply a measurement of the budgeted hours versus actual hours for each job. These were totaled each week and posted on the chart.

At first the numbers were not too impressive, so they had a meeting to get to the root causes and realized two things: (1) They needed to be more efficient in planning and staging work on site, and (2) Curtis needed to be selling the jobs at a higher cost, allowing for more man-hours. Both sales and production agreed to take steps to fix their part of the problem.

You could almost watch the productivity rise on the scoreboard since the day of the meeting. Production teams continued to meet regularly as team members kept coming up with new ideas to work more efficiently. The company was now beating budgeted hours by almost 20% each week.

The increase in productivity was also reflected in the fourth scoreboard, "Profitability," which showed the gross profit of the company on a weekly basis. Oscar had to work with their accountant to make sure she understood that they must have weekly reporting and that, in his words, "This is not an option." When the accounting firm knew what was expected of them, they did it. Curtis and Oscar established weekly gross profit goals and promised that for every week the company beat the goal, they'd cook hamburgers for everyone.

At first there wasn't much cooking, but during the past six months Curtis became as proficient at flipping burgers as the company had become at surpassing the goal. Curtis and Oscar were now discussing how to build a profit-sharing program based on the chart.

The fifth scoreboard simply measured FUN! Even Curtis, who used to be the yelling, get-to-work-or-else, my-way-or-the-highway type of manager, now saw this as very important. The team decided that they would put together a three-question survey that each employee would fill out on Fridays at the end of the day. The three questions were:

- On a scale of 1 to 10, how much fun did you have this week?

- What could the company do to make it more fun to work at Growing Dreams?

- What could you do to make it more fun to work at Growing Dreams?

The average employee rating for each week was then placed on the scoreboard, and the number had consistently improved even through the busiest seasons. Last week it had hit an all-time high of 9.2. Curtis looked forward to the day a perfect ten was registered.

The comments from the other two questions were typed up and placed on the training bulletin board each week, and they had introduced some valuable new programs and ideas into the company. Sales and profits were up. People were having fun. The company no longer had to look continually for new people to fill the positions of those who had quit. And of course Curtis savored his latest hirings: two new foremen had come to them from Cutter's Landscaping. They had been attracted by the training program at Growing Dreams, a great payback for the tire-slashing of ten months ago. Better yet, Curtis knew they would be attracting even more good people. The unity and efficiency developing within the company were becoming enviable.

The success the scoreboards and training had on sales had motivated Curtis to share his thoughts at a training session on "The Sales Process." When the day rolled around, the maintenance bay was buzzing as the Growing Dreams team came in and sat down. Several months ago Curtis had purchased folding tables and chairs to set up in the bay just for Training Challenge meetings. The easel with flip-chart paper was at the front of the room and the traditional "Rocky" theme music was playing as everyone entered, found a seat, and picked up a copy of Curtis's training outline from the table.

Oscar sat at the back of the room smiling proudly as he watched his younger brother pacing, nervously waiting to give his presentation. As the clock moved to 6:15 a.m., Curtis stepped to the front of the room and the crews jokingly gave him a standing ovation. It broke the ice and Curtis was ready to roll.

"ALL RIGHT YOU BUNCH OF SUPERSTARS!" Curtis called out loudly, confidently, and clearly. "We've got a lot to cover in thirty minutes. Pedro, would you like to read the company mission statement?" In advance, Curtis had asked Pedro, a newer employee, to perform their weekly training ritual of standing and reading the mission. After Pedro made his way through it in broken English, the rest of the team applauded wildly. His smile revealed his sense of accomplishment. "That mission is what we are all about,"

81

Curtis continued. "And all of you are making that statement a reality.

"We're going to talk about the sale process today. Here are the success factors we hope to accomplish:

- We understand how we get new customers.

- We understand how important it is to get referrals.

- Everyone understands the role they play in the process.

"Now here is a question for you. Why do we need sales?" Though the answers were fairly obvious, it did get people thinking about sales. Hands went up and Curtis wrote the responses on the flip chart.

"Without a sale, nothing happens."

"Sales are the way we grow."

"New sales move us into new areas."

By the time he was done there were nineteen positive responses on the flip chart.

"Great," Curtis continued as he turned to a blank sheet of paper. "Here is how we get those new sales. First the phone rings. . . ." He enthusiastically took them through the entire process and finished with the final check being collected and a referral being given. "As you see, everyone is important to the sales process," he concluded.

It was time to end the meeting with the "quote of the week." This week it had been assigned to a new foreman from

Cutter's. When Curtis called his name, he stood up and looked around the room. "For those who don't know me, my name is Pete. I used to work for the competition and in my five years of working there we never had a meeting like this.

"Now I know why you, I mean WE, are so successful. The quote I found really applies to this team. It is from UCLA basketball coach John Wooden, 'The main ingredient to stardom is the rest of the team.'" As the team cheered, Curtis felt his heart pounding. "OKAY, guys, it's 6:45. Let's get out of the gate by 7:00." In what seemed to be an instant, the room was cleared, chairs and tables put away, and the trucks were rolling toward the front gate. Oscar and Curtis stood in silence. "Great job, little brother," Oscar said, patting Curtis on the back.

"Oscar, you know who learned the most from that session? ME! Sitting down and going through the sales process reminded me of what I should be doing. And one of the things I need to do is hire another salesperson. If we're going to grow as owners, I can't be doing all of the sales. What do you think?"

"Put a plan together and I'll let you sell me on the idea," his older brother said, knowing he could be easily sold.

GROWING DREAMS

<u>GROWING POINT...</u>

Winners keep score. . . .

<u>BRAIN PROBE...</u>

I wonder how many ideas I can develop and put into action to measure and draw attention to the positive results that the team is achieving?

CHAPTER 9

Acting Lessons

"ACTING LESSONS!" Oscar shouted in disbelief. "Curtis, you're absolutely nuts. The guys won't go for it. They'll think you're nuts. No, they already know you're nuts. This will just confirm it. Tell me you're just kidding and we're not going to take acting lessons."

As usual, Curtis got his older brother's attention and had him frenzied before all the facts were on the table. "Oscar! Chill out . . . you're working on an Academy Award for the most spastic business partner in a landscaping company. All I said was that I had invited some professional actors to our Training Challenge session next Tuesday to teach us about role playing."

"Where did you meet professional actors?" Oscar still hoped there was a way to change his brother's mind before this got out to the rest of the Growing Dreams team.

"I went to a comedy club Saturday night. There was a group doing improvisations and I laughed all night long. You know how I get when I'm laughing: the right side of my brain kicks in and I start getting all these creative ideas. I thought how there is a need for our foreman, crew leaders and entire crew to think on their feet like this group doing improvs. After the show, I asked one of the group how she learned to do the improvs and comedy they were doing."

"Nice line!" Oscar said, not wanting to pass up a chance to jab his brother about his love life. "What did she look like? And did it work?"

"Gimme a break here, Oscar. I'm serious about this," Curtis said with a disgusted look that quickly turned to a smile. "Hey, I'm impressed! You thought quick, made up a line, went for a laugh. That kind of thinking is what we all need to know, whether it's to get a laugh, to get an idea accepted, or to calm an upset client and get him back on our side."

"All right, you have my attention." Oscar caught himself starting to get interested. "What did the girl say?"

"I couldn't believe it," Curtis continued. "She said they come to businesses and do classes on improvisation and role playing as a training tool! They've been to banks, accounting firms, real estate offices, and now they're coming to a landscape company. This Tuesday they'll take two hours and teach how to get loose, how to ad-lib, and how to carry out a successful role-playing training session. They gave me this format to use to write a couple of scenarios that we'll use on Tuesday."

Curtis handed the papers to Oscar and went up to the flip chart with marker in hand, ready to brainstorm. Oscar began reading from the paper. "It says here we need a title, a setting, the roles, and the director's questions. Do you know what these things are all about?"

"I sure do," the younger brother said with his enthusiasm building. "The first thing that the girl told me this weekend was to think up some specific situations that our team could find themselves in. She said a good question would be. . . ." Curtis turned to the flip chart and began to write, "What areas of our business should we practice before we find ourselves in those situations?"

"That's a good question," Oscar said now, his own enthusiasm growing to match his brother's. "It makes sense. Role playing can allow us to practice on a specific situation before it really happens. There's little doubt in my mind that we have lost employees and customers over the years by practicing on them rather than in a training session. So, let's list some specific situations. . . ."

The two brothers started firing off ideas with Curtis writing as fast as he could.

- Correcting an employee making a safety mistake

- Greeting a new employee on his first day

- A salesperson trying to close a sale

- A foreman with a problem on site with the work order

- A customer upset with a tree we just planted

- Firing an employee

- Hiring an employee

- Calming a disagreement between two employees

- Reprimanding an employee for diesel fuel instead of gas in the loader

- Greeting the customer when we arrive on site

- A disagreement on site with a salesperson, foreman and client

- A pre-job walk through

They soon realized that an endless number of situations could be role played and that each one of them could be just as important as the other. "Let's pick two of them," Curtis said. "I think one should be how to greet the new employee. We do a pretty good job of it, but when it gets busy, I've seen several rookies standing around on the first day not knowing where to go or what to do."

"Another one that some of Fernando's crew can relate to is the client not liking a tree. That just happened to them last week and I had to stop by the site and step between the client and Fernando," Oscar added. "It was not a pretty situation and I doubt we will be going back to that client anytime soon. I wish we would have practiced that one before it really happened."

"Okay, those are our two topics," Curtis said, seeming ready to hurry the process of writing role plays along. "I'll tell you what Jan said on writing the scenarios."

"Who's Jan?" Oscar said, knowing he had his brother going.

"That's the girl's name from the comedy club," Curtis replied, wanting to get on with the process. "That's who'll be here on Tuesday to teach the class. We need titles for the scenes."

"You got on a first-name basis pretty quick," Oscar said, wanting to continue his teasing. "Titles? How about . . . 'THE NEW GUY' and 'I DON'T LIKE THIS TREE.' Not real creative but they get the point across."

"Perfect," Curtis said. "Now the rest of the scene. You need to write a setting. That should be a two- or three-sentence explanation of the what, why and/or where of the scene. Does that make sense?"

"Got it."

"Next are the roles, the 'who' of the scene. She said you should add a little explanation of detail about each person, like why they might be feeling like they do, or why they are even in the scene. It gives the actors something to start with and relate to. Is that clear?"

"Got it," Oscar said, taking notes and ready to begin.

"Finally," Curtis continued, "the director's question. This is for the audience to pay attention to and discuss after the scene is played out. This is the most important part because it gives everyone the chance to learn and decide how the situation should or should not be handled. Do you understand that part of it?"

"Got it," Oscar said. "It shouldn't take us long to write these."

"Well, I was thinking maybe you could write them," Curtis said, getting out of his chair and moving toward the door. "I have an important meeting this evening with our role-playing consultant and I really do not want to keep her waiting. GOT IT?" Curtis ducked out the office door without getting hit by the flying copy of How To Win Friends and Influence People that his brother directed toward him.

UP GOES THE CURTAIN

The Tuesday morning training session was buzzing as the Growing Dreams team started arriving. Curtis had bought a CD of movie themes and ROCKY was playing loud as he stepped to the front of the room to introduce the guest instructor. "All right, ladies and gentlemen," he began. Perhaps a bit more nervous than in past sessions, he continued, "We are all going to become actors and actresses this morning. It will help us learn to communicate more effectively and Jan here tells me it is going to be fun. so . . . Jan . . . this group is all yours. . . ."

Jane Kendall stepped to the front of the room; her skill as an entertainer already had their attention. "ALL RIGHT! EVERYONE OUT OF THEIR SEATS. COME ON. COME ON! Get a PARTNER. NOW! High fives. Low fives. Both hands! High! LOW! Get up on your chairs. Now jump down. SPIN AROUND. High five. Low five. HAVE A SEAT!"

Curtis and Oscar couldn't believe their eyes. In twenty seconds she had the crowd loose and laughing. "Do you know why I did that?" she asked, turning the music down. "Because you have never done that before. That's why you're laughing. Smiling. We love doing things out of the ordinary, but back in school they taught us to conform, to color in the lines, to act like we were supposed to act. That conformity is a hindrance to communication. It causes us to draw inside ourselves, to fear speaking up or being different. I'm going to help you learn it's all right to be different, to do things out of the ordinary. ARE YOU READY?

There was a subdued and shocked "yes" from the audience, to which she replied, "NO. I mean are you REALLY

90

ready? You better get out of your seats and let me hear a great big . . . YES!"

Instantaneously they jumped from their seats and yelled, "YES!"

"I honestly believe I heard you that time," Jan said. "Now we can begin. It takes that energy to act, to learn, and to be willing to communicate. I'm going to take you through some basic warm-up exercises. The first one is learning to use your face to express emotion. Look at your partner and make the funniest face you can make."

As people began to follow the directive, deep and contagious laughter welled up and spilled into the room. Even the shy ones were laughing and getting involved. "Great job!" she continued. "Here's the next exercise. Add the funniest noise you can make to that face." The room was quiet for a moment. "I'M NOT KIDDIN' HERE! Let's hear some noises." The room exploded with cackling, whooping, beeping, and assorted other unidentifiable sounds. "You guys are doing great. Now let's start some real acting lessons."

For the next thirty minutes she taught them how to make an entrance, deliver lines, play off the other actors' leads, and stay in their roles until the scene was over. Curtis was excited that this training session had more energy and fun than any of the other sessions in the past.

"Now how about those scenarios you told me you wrote, Curtis?" Jan asked.

"Uh. Oh yeah. The scenarios. I think I gave those to you, Oscar, to get copied. Right?"

"Right, Curtis," Oscar said, getting up and shaking his head, knowing he was once again covering for his little brother. "I've got YOUR scenarios right here." Everyone took a copy and waited for Jan's instruction.

"You have two scenes in your hands that we could face on any given day here at work: greeting a new employee and talking with a concerned or upset client. Now I need some volunteers to play Scene 1. It was quiet for a moment and then one of the crew leaders said, "I'll be the new guy." He was followed by one of the new employees who raised her hand and said, "I'll be the foreman."

"Great!" Jan said. "Big round of applause for our actors. Here's the only rule. You do not stop acting until I say 'stop.' Keep communicating. Keep working at it. Get into your roles. Audience, you are the directors. Watch closely and we will discuss your recommendations when the scene is over. Are you ready? ACTION!"

For the next hour, Jan had the Growing Dreams team acting out the two scenarios and discussing possible solutions to each. They came up with ideas on how to make the new person feel welcome on his first day. Everyone gave input and one of the foremen wrote all the ideas down on the flip chart to implement and follow through on later. The upset-customer scenario gave specific ideas on how to talk to a customer and how to solve a problem without getting the salesperson involved. The foremen and crews realized that with practice they could learn to communicate with the customer and be a problem solver. Oscar and Curtis realized that role playing was going to be an important part of their weekly training sessions.

As the session drew to an end, Curtis stepped to the front of the crowd. "I'm proud of you guys. You did a great job with role playing. I think we can all be professional actors. I also think a standing ovation for our instructor would be a great idea." With that, the entire team jumped up and stood on their chairs, cheering and applauding loudly.

"Thanks. You guys are great," Jan said. "And since Curtis thinks he's ready for the stage, you all are invited to the comedy club this weekend to see him do a little improv with the actors there." Although her invitation was greeted with another standing ovation, Curtis looked scared.

"No problem," Oscar yelled. "He has been improvising all his life!"

GROWING DREAMS

<u>G</u>ROWING <u>P</u>OINT...

Do things out of the ordinary. It's all right to be different!

<u>B</u>RAIN <u>P</u>ROBE...

I wonder how many ideas I can develop and put into action that will move the entire organization out of our comfort zones to grow and learn?

CHAPTER 10

Hiring a Salesperson

Curtis was right on time for the meeting, which naturally surprised his older brother. "I thought we wouldn't get together until 9:30," Oscar said, keeping a straight face.

"What? We said we would meet at 9:00," Curtis replied as he sprang into the chair across from his brother's desk.

"I know," Oscar said, "but I've been conditioned to plan my day around you being a half hour late. I've scheduled nine a.m. to discuss the Meadow Lane project with Julio and Robert."

"Very funny. Now that you've had your little joke, can we talk about bringing on a salesperson so we can help him get started right? Believe it or not, I have sat down and put together some ideas and I want to move forward on them. Here they are." They were both excited about their company's potential with a full-time salesperson in place, but they were nervous about the costs and about handing over such important responsibilities. "Okay, Curtis, let's get to the important part first. What do we pay this person?"

"I knew you were going to ask that, Mr. Business Major. I called some of the people we met at the ALCA Conference and the conclusion is that there is no conclusion." Oscar raised an eyebrow and knew his little brother was ready to get on a roll.

"Some people said that straight salary is the best way to go," Curtis continued. "But the more I talked to them the more

I felt they were not happy with the sales totals their salespeople were turning in. I don't want to do straight salary. I want commission to give some incentive to sell more. Then other guys said they had their salespeople on straight commission. While it caused them to sell a lot, it also caused them to ignore paperwork and be poor team players. Most of the production staff was ready to kill them."

"We certainly don't need our new salesperson fighting with production," said Oscar. "We already have that with you as our salesperson," he added, not passing up a chance to give his brother a hard time. He knew Curtis and production worked great as a team. "Well, what's the plan, Curtis?"

"I want to do salary plus commission. We'll keep the salary just high enough to meet living expenses and get by. Then the commission kicks in and allows them to earn a great income—if they produce."

"We'll base the commission on the profitability of the job, right?" Oscar asked, now getting a little more serious.

"Nope," Curtis continued, "if we do that, we'll have the salesperson blaming the foreman for being inefficient and shrinking commissions. Then the foreman will retaliate by getting jobs done late so the salesperson will get paid less. We need to keep the salesperson focused on selling. That's when I sell the best—when I'm totally focused on my sales goal. That's what I want the new salesperson focused on."

"What keeps them from low-balling the job just to get a commission?"

"That's where you come in. This is just possibly our chance to get our money's worth out of you. You'll make sure our estimating and costing systems are clear and teachable to the new person, and we'll make sure they're followed.

"If a job comes in under our profit goals, we'll sit down and discuss it with the salesperson. If several jobs come in under profit, then we'll sit down and have a very serious talk. Besides, if the systems are set up front and we hire the right person, we shouldn't have to worry about the salesperson affecting profit on the job."

"Wow, I'm likin' it, little brother. I'm likin' it a lot. But the question is—how much?"

"Fourteen!"

"Fourteen? Did you just say fourteen? If you think you're going to get a salesperson for fourteen thousand dollars, you're crazy," Oscar said. "Just plain crazy."

"NO, 14%. At least for the first year. Everyone I talked to tries to keep their sales costs between 10% and 14% of their sales goal. This includes salary, commissions, vehicle, insurance, and all that stuff. So I guess whoever we pick, we should budget him in for 14% of his sales goal. Then the next year, if we pick the right person it could fall to 12% as he gets more established, and hopefully the next year it will drop to 10% or 11% if we pick the right person."

"So how do we pick the right person?" Oscar asked, beginning to believe that perhaps his brother wasn't crazy after all.

"I thought you would never ask," Curtis said, handing him an ad he had written.

INCREDIBLE OPPORTUNITY FOR AN ENTHUSIASTIC DESIGN/BUILD SALES-PERSON WITH A PROGRESSIVE AND AGGRESSIVE COMPANY THAT IS LEADING THE WAY IN ITS MARKET. CALL TO SEE IF YOU QUALIFY.

"Sounds a little bold, doesn't it, Curtis?" Oscar asked. "Why doesn't that surprise me?"

"You bet it is, and that's just what I want. A bold, aggressive, progressive individual that can come in here and make us have to work to keep up with him. I want him to call as well as send me a resumé. If he's content with just sending a resumé, then he'd probably be just as content sending a brochure to a client and waiting for something to happen."

"I want somebody with guts, Oscar. When they call in, I have some specific questions I'm going to ask. It'll cut down on the interview time if they qualify to come in." Curtis pulled out his list and began reading:

- *What makes you think you qualify to work for an aggressive and progressive company?* "I want them to sell me on themselves, Oscar."

- *Where are you presently working and do you know your company's mission statement?* "You know how important our mission statement is to us here. By asking them now, I'll get a chance to tell them ours."

- *How many books have you read in the past year?* "If they don't read or listen to tapes, I don't want them. When they come in for a live interview, I'll ask that question again and have them write a simple paragraph report on each of those books."

- *Do you belong to any professional organizations now or when you were in college?* "If they are not involved in the industry they work for, or work with, we don't want them either. You know how important the state association and ALCA have been to us. I want a person here who will be involved, not just collect a check and expect us to hand them a bunch of leads."

- *What will your spouse say about your making a change and coming here if you make the cut?* "We want to know the family relationship because we really are hiring a team if the person is married. I hope some guy says that his wife will say, 'It's about time you made a smart move.' A tough, supportive spouse is a great asset.

"I'll tell them I'll call back in a week. If I don't receive a thank-you card for the interview, they won't qualify." Oscar's eyes widened at his brother's tough stance. "This is bold stuff, Curtis. This is crazy stuff. I love it! It's efficient, too, and I think it'll help us find the person we want. But once we find this just-right person, how do we get him up and running after he's signed on? Got a plan?"

Now Curtis was really fired up. He knew he was about to close his sale and handed Oscar another report. "Here's one more piece of paper. This one is called 'First Things First.' It's a list of things I expect them to complete in the first month:

1. *Put on your work boots and spend a week with the crews.* "I want to build camaraderie between the salesperson and the crews."

2. *Take the foremen and their wives out to dinner.* "We'll pay for it. Again, I want them working together as soon as possible."

3. *Read two books: How to Win Friends and Influence People and Five Important Things.* "They'll read the first one to refresh their people skills and the second to keep themselves pumped for selling. I want them to start a habit of reading and learning."

4. *Write a press release announcing their hiring.* "I want their picture in the papers as much as possible."

5. *Watch a sales call with Curtis and then do a report on the strengths and weaknesses of the presentation.* "I want them to really think about our sales process. They'll need to be excited about Quality Performance Selling and the QPP."

6. *Set up fifteen appointments, and close at least five sales.* "They need to set some reachable goals and get some noticeable results."

7. *Get all of their goals for the month down on a 3 x 5 card.* "We're going to live goals around here on this sales team. Myself included."

Curtis pulled out a 3 x 5 card with several goals on it. The top goal said, "Hire the best landscape design/build salesperson possible." Oscar was impressed with the enthusiasm, time, and commitment his younger brother had put into preparing to hire their first salesperson. "Let's do it, Curtis. Let's run this ad and get some calls coming in."

"I'm really glad you said that, Oscar, because the ad is coming out in this evening's paper and I've already contracted with national magazines to run it." Curtis knew it was time to move fast as he leaped from his seat and shot through the door, laughing and ducking the copy of How to Win Friends and Influence People Oscar threw at him.

GROWING DREAMS

GROWING POINT...

Your approach to building the team will reflect the team you build.

BRAIN PROBE...

I wonder how many aggressive and progressive team-building approaches we can incorporate to attract aggressive and progressive team members?

CHAPTER 11

Closing the Gap Between Sales and Production

Growing Dreams Landscape Company's first salesman, Jeff Andrews, arrived at the job site to see how the finishing touches on the stone patio were coming. He found Henry, the company's newest landscape construction foreman, talking to the property owner. "That guy does this all the time," Henry said.

"Hi, Mrs. Bookman. Hey, Henry, the patio looks great," Jeff said.

"Mrs. Bookman was just telling me that we're supposed to clear out the wood line and mulch it. I don't see it in the work order." Jeff's face turned red when he realized he had forgotten to include the work in his paperwork and that Henry was badmouthing him in front of a customer. Although he wanted to strangle Henry, he kept his cool. He apologized to Mrs. Bookman and asked her to sign a change order. Then he asked Henry if he could clean out the brush and stop back to put the mulch down later. Henry nodded "yes" but flashed Jeff a disgusted look.

"I'll be right back, Mrs. Bookman," said Jeff. "Henry, would you help me fill out the paperwork?" When they reached the truck, both let out their frustration.

"IF I EVER HEAR YOU TALKING ABOUT ME LIKE THAT TO ONE OF MY CLIENTS AGAIN, I'LL MAKE SURE ONE OF US IS NO LONGER WORKING HERE." Jeff was so angry he felt his temples throbbing.

"LOOK, YOU SMOOTH-TALKING SNAKE-OIL SALESMAN, I'M SICK OF YOU SAYING ANYTHING JUST TO GET THE SALE, AND IF YOU KEEP IT UP YOU WON'T BE HERE," Henry replied.

"We'll finish this conversation back at the shop," Jeff said, realizing their shouts could be heard a block away.

As Henry and his crew stepped out of the truck, Oscar greeted them. "Hey guys, I hear the job looks great!" "What else did you hear?" Henry asked, preparing his defense in his head. "We'll get to that," Oscar said with a straight face. He asked the two crew members to unload the truck and trailer and get five yards of mulch ready.

"Si se puedo!" Both technicians answered enthusiastically.

"I love them guys," Oscar said turning to Henry. "You got a few minutes?"

"Sure, Big Boss," Henry said, trying to keep it light. "I suppose he told the whole story and it's all my fault, right?"

"Who said it had to be anybody's fault, Henry? The only thing I'm interested in is making sure it doesn't happen again. You can't fix history, but working together we can change the future."

Curtis and Jeff were in Curtis's office as Henry and Oscar entered. Clapping his hands loudly, Curtis began, "Gentlemen, thanks for pointing something very important out to Oscar and me today. The situation at Bookman's today reminds me of an important lesson my dear brother learned when we were starting out. We neglected to pass it on to you."

Oscar recalled, "Curtis asked me to fill in for his foreman and sent me out on a maintenance job with a one-man crew. But there was no way two people could finish the job in the time we were given. The radios didn't work, mowers kept breaking down, my 'crew' didn't speak English, and every time we tried to leave, the residents threatened to fire us."

"When Oscar returned that evening," added Curtis, "I thought he was going to beat me up like he did when we were kids. "When the dust settled, we learned several things: the foreman had been scared to tell the boss what to do, and I didn't understand what I was putting my crews through."

"And I didn't understand how hard it is to close the sale," said Oscar.

"It seems that we need a reminder of how the sales process works, how to move a sale into production, and how we represent Growing Dreams to customers," said Curtis. "This is an opportunity for us all to learn. Any idea who's going to lead this effort?" Jeff and Henry both squirmed in their seats for a few moments. Almost in unison they said, "I have an idea."

"Great!" continued Curtis. "Next Tuesday you guys will lead an expanded edition of the Training Challenge. You will creatively teach all of us the process we go through to sell a project. I want you to brainstorm with everyone on getting paperwork completed properly. We don't want another situation like today. Finish it up with a little role playing on how to respond to a customer comment such as 'The salesman said you would clean that wood line and mulch it.'"

"I would like to add a little to this assignment," Oscar said. "There's five yards of mulch on the back of your truck,

Henry. Jeff, since your schedule is open on Saturday morning, you will accompany Henry and his crew to Bookman's to spread the mulch. And while you're there, you might as well install the perennial border along that wood line that you sold her this afternoon. Nice sale!" Henry just looked at Jeff and shook his head with a hint of a smile, "You are incredible, Mr. Salesman."

"Jeff," Oscar continued, "you have an appointment Sunday afternoon. I want you to take Henry with you to observe so he can help explain the sales process Tuesday morning." That made Henry squirm even more in his seat. "And one more thing, I want you to take your wives out to the best restaurant and get to know each other. Curtis, give them your credit card."

"I have a question," Henry said. "What if we don't do it? What if I don't want to go on a sales call, or Jeff doesn't want to go out to eat with my wife and me?"

"I'm glad you asked," Curtis said, handing them both a piece of paper. "Here are the phone numbers of our top five competitors. If you don't think we're serious, then do me a favor and call one of these companies and ask them for a job. You'll do everybody here at Growing Dreams more good working for our competition with a negative attitude than you will working here."

Jeff looked up from the paper and then over toward Henry, "Do you like Italian food?" he asked, a dim smile crossing his face.

"I love Italian food," Henry responded, getting up and walking toward the office door. REALLY expensive Italian food. You better be here early tomorrow with your work boots on."

"You better have a tie on Sunday afternoon," Jeff responded as he followed him out the door.

"I don't even own a tie." The two men walked out, laughing about what they had gotten themselves into.

"Is there anything better than having a radical plan work out?" Oscar asked with a big sigh of relief. "It'll be interesting to see how the training goes Tuesday morning."

"Yeah, interesting. Very interesting," Curtis said, still holding his wallet in his hands. "But why did it have to be my credit card we gave them?"

GROWING DREAMS

GROWING POINT...

Radical plans will always produce radical results.

BRAIN PROBE...

I wonder how many ideas I can develop and put into action that will radically improve the company?

CHAPTER 12

Systems for Success

Curtis did a little victory dance and spiked his clipboard over his shoulder. "That's seven crews out by 7:07. Not too bad and we've been pretty consistent at doing that day after day," he said, looking over at his brother for approval.

But Oscar was using his clipboard for more than throwing. His pencil was working out some simple calculations that had his interest going beyond what his brother was excited about. Seven crews, totaling twenty people times seven minutes a day equaled 140 minutes or almost two and a half hours! He multiplied that times an estimated $35 dollars an hour, the time they were losing not being on the job, and wrote "$87.50" on his clipboard.

"Curtis, if I opened my wallet and pulled out $87.50, placed it on the ground here in front of us, and put a match to it right now, what would you think?"

"I'd think you're crazy, but I already think that, so what's your point?"

"My point is the seven minutes of delay just now. When those twenty people got out of here at 7:07 instead of 7:00, we burned up $87.50 or more."

Curtis laughed, picked up his clipboard, and commented that Oscar was getting a little "anal." He stopped in his tracks when Oscar followed it up with, "What if I set a match to $22,750.00?"

"Then it would confirm my feelings that you're crazy and I'd beat you with this clipboard. What are you getting at, Oscar? Why are you throwing all of these numbers around?"

Oscar had made a discovery as he stood there watching the crews scurry to get loaded and out the gate. He realized that each of the crew leaders had his own way of getting ready in the morning. They all had little things that they did to load their trucks, get the needed tools, instruct their crew, and head for the front gate. Even though it looked efficient and seemed to be working, he knew it could be better. If improving this one process could save the company over $22,000.00 a year, how many other simple things could be improved and yield the same savings?

"Curtis, we're losing over $22,000.00 every year by not creating a unified approach to getting those crews out of here each morning. If we could just get them out seven minutes faster, we could add that money right to our bottom line. And that's just one example. How many more seven-minute time segments could we save if we were taking a more systematic approach to running our business?"

Oscar had captured his business partner's attention. He was talking profits, one of Curtis's favorite subjects. "Well, it sounds as if we're finally getting some payback from that college education of yours. Tell me more," he said.

"It doesn't take a college education to figure it out, Curtis. We're doing a lot right around here. Our crews work hard at doing the right things and serving the customer. They seem to work well as a team, the training is going well, and they're focused on the customer. We're just missing an opportunity to be even more efficient. Let me talk about something you understand: food. How many times a day are you at a McDonald's?"

"I might stop once, on occasion twice. What does that have do to with us saving $22,000?"

"I read a book about McDonald's last week. Think about it, Curtis. They're the same everywhere you go. They're systematized and teach those same systems to each and every employee. The systems are in a manual that every manager uses. They're expected to know the systems, to adhere to the systems, and to offer suggestions on improving the systems. That's why McDonald's has been able to grow and succeed. Systems are an important part of any great company's success. They should be our next step in building Growing Dreams, Curtis. We have to develop, document, enforce, and continually improve on the systems that help the company to function!"

"You're really making me hungry, Oscar."

"Get serious, Curtis." This is the big opportunity for us."

"How do you suggest we approach this opportunity?"

"The same way we have in the past when we wanted to make an improvement. We have a meeting and get everyone's input. Think about it, Curtis. Every time we get the crews together and ask for ideas, they respond with more information than we could ever generate on our own. We'll have a 'SEVEN OUT BY SEVEN' meeting. It'll be an opportunity for all of the crews to come together and share their 'best practice' ideas for getting out of the gate in the mornings. This meeting will be a little different, though. We're always good at writing ideas down on the flip chart, but where do they go from there? That's the step we're missing, taking them from the flip chart and documenting them into a Growing Dreams systems manual. I'm going to work with Michelle this afternoon to put together a format that we'll use for documenting each system. This format will then be organized into a three-ring binder that is always available in the office and becomes part of the orientation package for new hires as well as old veterans. It'll be our play book! Next Tuesday evening we'll bring in lots of McDonald's hamburgers to emphasize the effectiveness of systems, and we'll write the 'OUT BY SEVEN' system as a group. Between now and then, I'll give each of the seven crews a blank sheet of paper and tell them to come to the meeting with ideas on what should go into this system."

"What if they don't fill it out?" Curtis asked.

"I'll threaten them with standing and singing "Wild Thing" like Jimmi Hendrix! Now I've got work to do," Oscar said, buzzing by Curtis and then stopping, turning around and saying, "Bring me back a cup of coffee will ya? I know where you're headed."

The meeting room smelled like a McDonald's restaurant as the crew gobbled down the hamburgers. Oscar had written "7 out by 7" on the flip chart with a thick-line black magic marker. His big, bold strokes conveyed the importance he was attaching to the concept. Moving to the front of the room, he asked everybody to find a seat. He moved quickly, like a man on a mission. handing out the template that he and Michelle had worked on. It would be used to document each system that was created from here on out and already had a thick, three-ring binder labeled "Growing Dreams, Systems for Success!"

The meeting began with a review of the system format form. He went over each section, explaining the title of the system; why the system was needed; the detailed, numbered steps of the system; who authored the system; and what the consequences for non-compliance would be for the individual or company. He added that anyone was able to fill out one of these forms and submit it to Michelle to be typed and then reviewed. After review and acceptance, it would be placed in the systems manual and a copy given to every crew leader to review with their crews. There were a few questions, but everyone seemed to understand the process and agree with it.

"Now I hope you all took me seriously about doing your homework because I really don't want to hear any of you frogs try to sing." Oscar was greeted by seven crew leaders, each holding up pieces of paper with ideas on them. He turned the pages of the flip chart to reveal the following question:

"What is the most effective step-by-step process that the crews of Growing Dreams can use to consistently get out of the gate by seven each morning?"

Oscar had learned in a creativity seminar that the first step in brainstorming is to create a clear and concise focus question that everyone understands and that will keep the group on track with its ideas. He also learned that at least in the idea-generating portion there are no bad ideas. He was greeted with some of the following suggestions, which he quickly wrote down on the flip chart:

- Keep Curtis away until 7:30.

- Turn all of the clocks back by 15 minutes ! ! ! !

- Keep the crews the same.

- Schedule better so everyone knows their assignment the evening before.

- Load up at night when it's less hectic.

- Have the trucks pointed toward the front gate.

- Have the crew leaders come in before the crews to plan and prepare.

- Give lunch money to every crew out by 7:00.

- Provide all the crews with their own tools.

- Call in by 3:00 the previous day for any special request or concerns on a job.

- Make each crew leader responsible for his crew being on time.

- Keep score and see who has the longest streak of being out by 7:00.

- Reward for team perfection each week.

- Penalize any crew out after 7:00 with the task of washing Curtis's truck. (That was one of Curtis's ideas.)

When the idea-generating exercise was complete, Oscar had three full pages of ideas. They then began to sort through the list and cross out the ones that were not workable. Curtis's truck washing was one of the first to go. When the exercise was complete, they had strategically put together a list of ten steps that would ensure that "7 were out by 7" each morning. The steps included loading the night before, specific parking locations, afternoon call-ins, and all crews in on time, with the final step being Oscar cooking hot dogs on Friday if the week was 100% out by 7:00. Michelle had been busy typing the notes into her laptop as the crews finalized the procedure; she asked for five minutes to print the results and get a copy for everyone.

The crews were all feeling pretty important; they had worked through the process and been included in something that was going to help the company. As Oscar looked down the list, he discovered a phenomenon about writing systems. In making the ten steps, they had created the need for other systems to be written. While Michelle was making the copies, Oscar suggested that they create one more list of other systems that could be written and asked for volunteers to write them.

The five-minute exercise turned into fifteen minutes and three more pages of ideas:

- Unloading procedure in the evening

- Gassing and cleaning trucks

- Scheduling work (Curtis was volunteered for this one.)

- Call-in procedures

- Equipment repair procedure

- Excused absence procedures

- Change orders procedures

- Accident reports

- From gate to curb

- From curb to gate

- Job set up

It became clear that there were infinite numbers of procedures that could be addressed. They decided to take the top seven; each crew would work on writing a procedure and plan to present it next Friday when Curtis and Oscar fired up the grills.

Michelle handed everyone a copy of the system that they had compiled that evening and ceremoniously put the first system into the "Growing Dreams Systems For Success" book. Oscar thanked everyone for participating and ended the meeting by volunteering Curtis to recite the mission statement.

"WOW! When you get excited about something, you get it done," Curtis told his brother. But Oscar was once again busy scratching some numbers onto his clipboard and then punching them into his calculator.

"I just discovered another way the company could save an additional $22,000.00," Oscar said with enthusiasm.

"Man I'm all ears," Curtis said. "You made a believer out of me on this systems stuff."

"Well, this one might be a little tougher. It would mean writing a system to get you to stop at McDonald's only once a day as opposed to two or three times." This time Oscar did his own little victory dance and then spiked his clipboard!

GROWING ✔ DREAMS

GROWING POINT...

Systematically document the processes of the company.

BRAIN PROBE...

I wonder how many ideas I can develop and put into action that will allow the company to create, understand, and adhere to the systems that help the company successfully function?

CHAPTER 13

Sharing the Success

"Hey, Curtis, it's been our best year ever, at least that's what you told me," Oscar said, sitting down across from his brother. "So why don't you let your face know it? What's the problem, my little sibling? Are you afraid somebody is going to ask you to plow snow this evening? You know the guys won't allow you in the trucks anymore."

"Oscar, something's missing," Curtis replied monotonously as he turned his desk chair around and stared out the window at the snow coming down. "Something just doesn't feel right about our business and I can't put my finger on it."

"What's not right?" Oscar laughed. "We just had the fifth straight year of record sales. Did you hear me? RECORD SALES! And next year is going to be even better. We did what we had been wanting to do for a long time . . . DOUBLE DIGITS net profit. The bank likes that, and it doesn't hurt my feelings either. We have the best crews in the city, if not all of the state, and they're doing a great job running the day-to-day, holding weekly training sessions, and ensuring customer satisfaction. What's not right?"

Curtis slowly turned around and looked at his brother. "Oscar, have you ever walked through the employee parking lot?"

"Every day for the last five years. Why?"

"What do you see?" Curtis asked, keeping the distant look in his eyes and not really needing an answer.

"Is this a trick question? I see cars," Oscar said, starting to get a little disgusted and worried about his brother's mood.

"What kind of cars?"

"Curtis! I don't know. All kinds of cars. Why?"

"Oscar, I see old, rusty, secondhand cars. That's what I see. Why are those cars parked in the parking lot if we have the best crews in the country? And do you know how many crew members have gotten divorced in the past two years?"

"You're really starting to worry me, Curtis. I have no idea, but I suspect you do."

"We've had four divorces and who knows how many break-ups," Curtis said, turning back around to watch the snow continue to fall. "And how about you and me, Oscar? We haven't had a serious relationship in years. The only marriage we can think about is that we are married to this business. The business is going great; you're right. But I think the thing that's missing is quality of life. For you, for me, and for every one of those great guys out there that have committed their lives to our business. Something has to change. We've got to develop a rewards process and help everyone make more in less time."

Oscar wasn't sure what to say or how to answer. "Curtis, I think we reward the guys pretty well. How about the year-end bonus we gave out at the Holiday Party? We paid a total of $45,000.00 to twenty-one guys. That's pretty good money. Isn't that a reward?"

"Did you see their faces when they opened their checks, Oscar? I did. Their faces said they were expecting more. They are all too loyal to say anything, but I saw it. We need to teach them how to make more. We need to show them where the bonus comes from, not just throw money at them. I want to pay them more, and I want them to get it without sacrificing their personal lives to get it. We need to understand and define what success really is. It's not just about becoming the biggest, boldest, richest. It's about enjoying the process over the accomplishment. We'll learn how to make money and have an enjoyable personal life at the same time. That's success. We'll somehow develop a program that will SHARE THE SUCCESS." Then the room fell quiet.

"Oh no," Oscar said as he saw that all-too-familiar look come into Curtis's eyes just before a wild idea was about to be born.

"THAT'S IT!" Curtis yelled, jumping up and clapping his hands. "THAT'S IT. We'll create an entire philosophy called 'SHARE THE SUCCESS' – S.T.S. We'll incorporate help from outside sources, like our accountant and some industry experts. We'll ask the team to help with it and it will be revolutionary." Curtis was now standing on top of his desk; his brother stared in disbelief.

"I'm not sure I want to ask," Oscar joked, "but where do we start?"

"We'll start by first defining success. Just like we created our mission statement to guide the company, we'll create a definition of success for the entire company. In one of the Training Challenge sessions, we'll try to define success. We'll build off this definition by determining what motivates people. We'll then bring in the accountant because we need to know the numbers in a timely fashion, not after the month is over, but right now while we can do something about it. If he can't get us that information, we'll seek out somebody who can. Then we'll educate. How many of the crew do you believe really know how the company makes or loses money?

"I'm not sure. But now that you mention it, I overheard Frederico and José talking about how you probably get to keep at least 50% of everything the company sells."

"That's what I'm talking about, Oscar. If they're thinking that, and I am sure most employees are, let's tell them the truth. Let them see how we risk everything each year to try to keep 10% of everything we sell. Let's educate on the financials and share information. We don't even need to go all the way to net profit. Let's just start with revenue minus materials and labor to get us to gross profit. That's all the crews can help control anyway. I'll start at the training session on Tuesday to introduce the idea and see what they think. Then as a group we'll start to develop the program.

"We'll start paying quarterly or maybe even monthly bonuses on hitting gross profit goals. I'll never pay out another throw-money-away Christmas bonus. The team members are going to be in control of their destinies, and they alone will determine how much they make in bonuses, not you or me. We are going to SHARE THE SUCCESS.

"Once the numbers are understood, Oscar, we'll start talking about efficiency. What if every one of the crew worked normal hours, you know forty to forty-five hours a week, and no more? What if we could base a bonus on just the minimum number of hours instead of thinking the only way to work is around the clock? Do you know how many hours Frederico has worked this week? Seventy-two hours, and he'll be going out this evening to plow all night. I believe we can change that."

"HOW?" Oscar asked, starting to get caught up in new possibilities. Frederico likes the overtime."

"Does he like the overtime, or does he like the rewards that overtime brings him? We need to find that out. We all need to realize that we can make more money by working smarter, not just harder."

"Okay, but how are you going to develop such a plan?" Oscar asked, watching the idea grow in his little brother's head.

"I don't know yet, but I'll make some calls. There have to be some people around the country that can give us direction. What we need is a compass to point us in the right direction, and then we can figure out the details." Curtis stood up and walked over to the white erasable board that had hatched many ideas in the past years. "Oscar, let's you and I start now and list the criteria for a the Share The Success program." He picked up the marker and began to write:

- IT IS SIMPLE AND EASILY UNDERSTOOD. ("Even by the owners," Oscar added. "Get serious with this," Curtis needled back.)

- THE ENTIRE COMPANY BECOMES EDU-CATED ON THE KEY FINANCIALS OF THE BUSINESS.

- IT IS BASED ON WORKING SMARTER, NOT HARDER . . . CREATING EFFICIENCY AND SYSTEMS.

- THE CUSTOMERS BENEFIT AND RECEIVE THE QUALITY THEY DESERVE.

- IT IS PAID OUT IN NINETY DAYS OR LESS FROM THE TIME THE TEAM EARNED IT.

- IT REFLECTS AND DRIVES US TOWARD THE COMPANY MISSION STATEMENT.

- IT DEVELOPS OPEN COMMUNICATION AND TEAMWORK BETWEEN ALL THE DEPART- MENTS OF THE COMPANY.

- IT IS EASILY MEASURED AND TRACKED

- IT IS THE PHILOSOPHY WE RUN OUR BUSI- NESS BY, NOT JUST SOMETHING DIS- CUSSED WHEN WE ARE SUPPOSED TO PAY A BONUS.

- IT IMPROVES THE QUALITY OF LIFE FOR EVERYONE INVOLVED IN THE COMPANY.

Curtis set the marker down and looked at the list of statements. "That's it, Oscar . . . that list is the compass. We just have to move in that direction."

"I'm with ya, Curtis," Oscar said, standing up and giving his brother a high five.

"Oscar, this is the best idea I've had since I decided to hire you full time," Curtis said, his spirits lifting appreciably.

"What do you mean you decided to hire me? I decided to come help you. Where are you going?"

"I think I'm going to begin a little quality of life this evening. I have a young lady I would like to discuss sharing some success with." Curtis winked as he put his coat on and headed for the door.

GROWING DREAMS

GROWING POINT...

Companies must S.T.S.—
Share the Success—in order
to continually be successful.

BRAIN PROBE...

I wonder how many ideas I
can develop and put into
action that will create energy
and opportunity for everyone
in the company through
recognition of their efforts?

CHAPTER 14

Keeping the Good Ones

Oscar, staring out the window, wondered where they'd gone wrong. "It seems like the perfect place to work," he thought. "We have the Training Challenge in full swing and almost everyone participates. The company is profitable and bonuses are being paid. There are benefits, paid vacations, great projects to work on, and effective meetings. What is it? Why would someone like Tom leave the company?" Oscar was feeling betrayed and confused, and the more he thought about it, the angrier he became.

"Hey Oscar!" Curtis stuck his head in the door and yelled the same way he'd been yelling since he could first say his older brother's name almost twenty-two years ago. "Sold another one! ! ! $18,000.00 with a 50% deposit and we won't need to be on the site until late next month." Curtis hesitated and then walked into the office and sat down. He could tell by his brother's face that something was up. "Hey, didn't you hear me say another sell? I know that makes the bean counter in you happy, so why don't you let your face know it? What's up?"

"Tom quit," Curtis said, slapping the top of his desk, standing up and then sitting back down in his chair. "Can you believe it? That guy's been with us for three years. He's moved from technician to crew leader to foreman. He was one of the highest-paid guys here, with lots of responsibility and a company vehicle. Why would he leave?"

Now Curtis could feel the anger. "Where's he going? What'd he say?"

"He came in here before going out on his route and gave a two-week notice. You're not going to believe what I'm going to tell you. He said he'd been talking with Cutter's off and on all winter and he'd finally decided to make the move."

Now Curtis was really angry. "Wait a minute. Talked with Cutter's all winter while we were carrying him on full salary? While he sat around here, had it easy, complained about plowing snow and clean-up work on the equipment? And now spring is here, we're moving into full season, and he decides to quit? Does he think he's doing us a favor by giving a two-week notice? Oscar, I'm not mad that this turkey is leaving; I'm mad that we were stupid enough to keep him around in the first place. We have a great company here with opportunities to grow, training, benefits, and incentives. We have to make sure this doesn't happen to us again. Any ideas?"

Oscar could see the ideas brewing in his brother's head and knew the question was the beginning of a process that would make the company better. "I don't know about ideas yet, but I pulled some information on how many people left us in the past year. You might find it interesting. We had as many as twenty-eight employees last year at peak. I counted how many W-2's we issued last year; we had thirty-eight counting you and me. That means throughout the year we had ten employees leave us. I don't know if that's good or bad, but that's the number. Here's another interesting fact. We're geared up with twenty-five people right now, and if you keep selling we'll be up to probably thirty-five before the end of the month, but out of those twenty-five, twenty are coming back from last year. I think that's pretty good . . . 80%. The turnover must be taking place in 20% of the employees. That's all I have right now. What do you have in mind?"

Curtis was deep in thought. "We have to push that 80% up to 90% or higher next year. Just think how much stronger we'll be and how much more prepared for the spring. We also need to get to work and find out what other companies around the country are doing. Let's make some phone calls to some of our ALCA connections. Why don't you get onto the ALCA website and see what you can find on employee retention? I'm going to put the managers to work finding out why 80% of our work force came back this spring and how can we use that information to get it to 90% and higher. Let's meet at the end of the week, see what we found, and put a plan into action. I got one more thing to do."

"What's that?" Oscar asked as he watched his partner move toward the door.

"I'm going to visit Tom on the job site, do a quick exit interview, and promote Fernando up to foreman. Then I'll give Tom a ride back to the office, help him get his things together, and tell him to find a ride home. I don't need two weeks of cockiness around here. It'll do more harm than good."

Curtis was high fiving the managers as they came into the meeting. He was excited about building a team that wanted to be part of the "Growing Dreams Experience." That's what he put on the top of the agenda for the meeting, "CREATING THE GROWING DREAMS EXPERIENCE."

Curtis began with an update on Tom's exit interview. "Here's what this guy told me. He didn't like the way the company was being run. He thought we were taking advantage of everybody, making them sit in training meetings, working for the incentive program, and taking money out of checks for health benefits and 401K. I won't even tell you what he said about the high fiving and 'standing around the campfire and singing Kum-Ba-Yah.' He said he wanted to go to a businesslike company he thought he could move forward with. This is coming from a guy that did not volunteer to teach one training session last year, lost eight out of the ten people we turned over, didn't come to the picnic, and refused to shovel sidewalks. My conclusion is that we were stupid for keeping him. He should have been fired long ago and we didn't see it."

"Managers, what did you find out from the rest of the team? What brought them back this year?"

The managers all began to laugh. "What's so funny?" Oscar asked, looking around the table.

"The reasons they wanted to come back are the very reasons that Tom wanted to leave. They love the training, benefits, incentives, and camaraderie of the team. Every one of them said they like the people they work with. It's a family. They added that they thought they could move into management positions in the future and that the company would continue to grow. Several said the only reason they would leave is if things changed and we no longer did the training, incentives, and monthly meetings. Overall, people love this place."

Now Curtis and Oscar were laughing in disbelief. They knew they had accomplished what they had set out to do several years ago, create a company that people loved. However, there was still more to do. No resting on past laurels.

"Here's what I found out," Oscar said. "ALCA companies that I called said they had anywhere from 20% to 100% turnover. One of the companies mentioned that they might be as high as 200%, but only because they hire a lot of temporary help. So our 20% turnover for the year is not bad,

especially since most of it came from Tom's crews. A lo[
companies would love to have had 80% of their workforce
returning, so our goal of more than 90% is an audacious one."

"That's why I like it ! ! ! !" Curtis yelled, standing up
and clapping his hands. "Settle down!" Oscar said, before you
chase the entire management team away, including me. The
rest of the team laughed as Oscar continued. "One of the
owners I called said that he had heard in a recent seminar that
the reason some employees leave is they never should have
been hired in the first place. He told me about a concept called
'hiring by T-E-C.' The 'T' stands for traits, the 'E' for
experience, and the 'C' for chemistry. He said chemistry is the
most important of the three. If an employee doesn't mix with
the rest of the team, you've made a bad hire."

"That's why Tom is no longer here," Curtis said. "The
chemistry was wrong; he didn't fit in."

"Exactly," Oscar continued. "He also didn't have the
traits or the attitude we look for in a good team member, which
is the second most important thing to consider in hiring a
person. Although Tom had experience and knowledge, those
are the least important attributes of a good hire. The experience
and skill can be acquired if the traits and chemistry are there.
Most companies make the mistake of hiring for skill first and
then hoping the traits will develop and the chemistry will just
miraculously appear. It's time to rethink our process of
recruiting and hiring. This is the best way to reduce turnover
and improve employee retention."

"I'm really impressed with this, Oscar. This is huge.
This could make all the difference in the world, guys. Count
me in on anything that'll deep-six that stress that disgruntled
employees are so good at creating," Curtis said. "We can't

leave here until we take this information and put a plan together. Based on everything we just talked about, what we have learned in the past, and what we know we need for the future, what's the answer to the following question?"

Curtis walked over to the easel and wrote the following:

"WHAT WILL WE DO TO IMPROVE EMPLOYEE RETENTION TO MORE THAN 90% AND MAKE SURE EVERYONE ON THE TEAM UNDERSTANDS THE GROWING DREAMS EXPERIENCE?"

The team began brainstorming, and within an hour, they had developed the list that every one of the managers committed to following through on.

1. We have developed a list of criteria on the chemistry and traits we are looking for in new hires.

2. We have developed our recruiting efforts to attract people that meet this list of criteria.

3. We have improved our hiring process to include testing and exercises that will determine if a candidate qualifies to work for our company.

4. We have created an orientation program for new employees that introduces the company philosophy and establishes a career path for each individual.

5. We take the approach of "Hiring slowly and Firing quickly" to reduce bringing on the wrong team member and delaying the inevitable.

6. We continue to place an importance on training and skill development that provides opportunity for every team member to gain the experience he needs.

7. We make a practice of hiring more people than we need to and make cuts as necessary, keeping the people that fit best into the team.

8. We are committed to cutting turnover in half and bringing back more than 90% of our team each year.

The team felt a sense of accomplishment as they stood, closed their notebooks, and knew their assignments. Oscar and Curtis thanked them all for their input as they left the meeting room and headed back out to the field. "Man, I do believe we're getting pretty good at turning lemons into lemonade," Curtis said.

"You know what else was happening back there?" Oscar added. "We're developing some leaders. They're not there yet, but they're starting to take the company and their careers seriously. What we need to do now is find the right approach to enhance their leadership skills."

Curtis knew his brother was right. They had done so much to build Growing Dreams and the people who formed the team behind it. If the company was going to continue to grow, the leaders that could one day replace Curtis and Oscar had to be formed. "We've got to find the right approach to leadership development. A seminar or course or bungee jumping or something. The future of the company depends on it.

GROWING  DREAMS

<u>GROWING POINT...</u>

Create a culture that attracts and retains the best people.

<u>BRAIN PROBE...</u>

I wonder how many ideas I can develop and put into action that will create the best possible career experience for everyone?

CHAPTER 15

We Be Jammin'!

"WE BE JAMMIN'! WE BE JAMMIN'! WE BE JAMMIN'!" The reggae tune blasted from a boom box as four foremen danced through the office. Curtis, Oscar, and Jeff Andrews, their rookie salesman, sat with stunned expressions before following the foremen into the training room. "You guys are nuts," Jeff said as he sat down.

"You're absolutely right, Jeffrey!" said Henry Knock, Growing Dreams veteran foreman. "Let's get this meeting started. Billy, José, Mark, and I started going over everything we learned at Leadership Jam on the way home this weekend. "You always have us teach you what we learned when we come back from seminars. We not only learned a lot, but we've come up with some great goals and plans. We need your input." Oscar and Curtis, amazed, looked at each other. Here was their forty-five-year-old foreman who hated meetings, accountability, and salespeople now talking about goals and plans.

Henry clapped his hands and got started. "I'll give a quick overview and then Billy, José, and Mark will present the game plans they've created. The first thing we learned about was creating an exciting atmosphere. When we walked into the meeting room, it was like nothing we had ever seen: music, balloons, and decorations all over the place. We played crazy games and won these gold medals.

"We spent a lot of time talking about creating an exciting atmosphere. When the energy is high and everyone is working as a team, it makes life a lot easier for everyone. Our customers even get excited. We're committed to help create that atmosphere." Curtis and Oscar could see this was not just a "seminar high." Something had happened to Henry.

"The next thing we discussed was the mindset of a leader," Henry continued. "This helped me because I always thought the mindset of a leader was to make everyone afraid to talk back to you. I learned that's why people leave my crew and why I'm always having to train someone new. Here's a handout that Billy typed up." Billy, who hadn't talked for more than fifteen minutes at a stretch in his two years at Growing Dreams, presented a great mini-seminar on the Intensity Model:

DISCOVERING THE MINDSET OF A LEADER

The commonality of all leaders is INTENSITY OF FOCUS. Intensity is understood through the following model:

- **INITIATIVE:** Doing what needs to be done without being told to do it. This means developing insight and understanding that allows a leader to make good decisions.

- **NEGOTIATION:** Being able to reach fair and concise terms with employees, vendors, customers, and other leaders.

- **TENACITY:** Developing a mindset to complete the task without fail, whether it is a landscape project or a personal goal.

- **ENTHUSIASM:** Developing the charisma to make people want to follow you.

- **NEVER PANIC:** Maintaining composure in difficult situations. Many a leader has lost the respect of the team after losing his temper.

- **SUCCESS:** Understanding that success comes the instant you believe you are a success. When you humbly believe in yourself and your ability, you can help others to believe in themselves.

- **IT TURNS YOU ON:** Getting and staying energized through the INTENSITY model. When you are energized, you naturally energize those around you. An energized person functions at peak performance.

"Great job, Billy," said Henry with a high five. "You should have heard him at the Leadership Jam. We all were taught how to take the Intensity Model and put it into a personal game plan called 'Professional Consistency' that we'll monitor every day to help stay on track as leaders and individuals. The next thing we learned were the Fundamental Business Issues, or FBIs: market, teamwork, training, systems, cost control, and rewards.

"These six words were repeated so many times that I heard them in my sleep last night. They're the six issues that great companies focus on. We talked with other foremen and managers and shared ideas, which led to a very important part of the Leadership Jam. Everyone put together their own Business Contribution Plan, or BCP. We'll spend the rest of the meeting presenting our individual plans," Harry continued.

"The BCP challenged us to create an 'AIM'— Awesome Incredible Milestone. It's a big-picture goal in each of the six areas I just told you about. Then we put together a step-by-step game plan on how we would reach this AIM. We decided that each of us should concentrate on one FBI."

By now the brothers' heads were spinning with BCPs, FBIs and AIMs. They weren't sure what it all meant, but they were excited that their foreman were taking the initiative. Curtis was hoping this wasn't all a dream.

"My main focus will be on the first fundamental business issue—the market," Henry continued. "Jeff, since that shouting match you and I had on that job site a couple weeks ago, I've been thinking how bad that could have made us look as a company. I don't think we understand how important the customer's perception is in helping our business to grow. That's why I want to tackle this one." He handed out a form with his written AIM at the top followed by his game plan and a list of realistic goals for accomplishing it. "My AIM is 'Every team member at Growing Dreams is clear on the expectations of every customer we serve and understands the importance of exceeding those expectations.'"

"Amen," Oscar shouted, bowing reverentially. "Thank you, Brother Oscar," Henry said in his best preacher voice. "Here's the first item in my game plan: 'Develop a list of the top ten things we can do to exceed customers' expectations, then put it on posters around the shop and in the trucks and talk about it in meetings.' Jeff, I'll need your help along with everyone in the company. I want to have it done before the month is out so I can get points."

"We're in the LAPS program!" Billy jumped up. "We're competing to see who gets the most points each month for accomplishing a list of things that leaders should be doing in their companies. We decided last night that our company is going to win! My focus," he continued proudly, "is going to be on teamwork and my AIM is: 'We have found the most innovative ways to recruit, hire, orient, and communicate with individuals to create a great team at Growing Dreams.'" He then presented his six-step game plan to begin doing this. Everyone applauded.

Next was José, who jumped up and handed out his BCP. "I'm going to focus on training and my AIM is: 'As a company, we have continued our Training Challenge using a great variety of tools, from role playing to hands-on skills development, that has everyone in the company contributing to improving quality and improving themselves.'"

Mark took the floor next. "My focus is on systems. My AIM is, 'Every individual on the Growing Dreams team understands the importance of following through on paperwork and procedures that allow the company to operate at peak efficiency.'" The room was silent. "What's the problem?" Mark asked.

"Well, it's just um . . . it's just that you're the biggest offender of not handing in paperwork," Curtis said, unable to repress a laugh. "I know!" Mark said. "That's because I never realized how important it was until the Leadership Jam this weekend. Now I have a plan to help me and everyone else follow through on paperwork. Here it is. . . ."

When Mark's presentation ended, the four managers stood, clearly impressed, but the room fell quiet when Curtis stood and spoke. "Oscar and I have been wrestling with this business since we were kids. We've made some strides toward becoming a real business the last few years, but we really didn't have everyone on board. We sent four employees to the Leadership Jam and they came back leaders. Together we're going to take this company to new heights!"

Walking around the table and giving everyone a hearty, congratulatory handshake, he continued, "Let's go. Steaks are on me tonight!" He then turned to Oscar and said with deep satisfaction, "We've just looked into the future and it looks . . . well, it looks great!"

GROWING DREAMS

GROWING **P**OINT...

Developing great leaders today produces a great future.

BRAIN **P**ROBE...

I wonder how many ideas I can develop and put into action to grow the individuals who will lead the company in the future?

CHAPTER 16

A Dream Come True

"Dinner? Why would Frank Cutter want to have dinner with us?" We haven't liked each other since we first met on the cul-de-sac when he was trying to steal the Hamleys from us. Remember that?"

"I sure do," Oscars said. "Even at eight years old you were a know-it-all. Always ready to get in somebody's face. It's a good thing I came back into the business and straightened you out."

Curtis and Oscar smiled as the reminisced. That day seemed like yesterday. Had twenty-five years really passed? Curtis could still see the two of them bolting from the school bus, and he could hear himself pleading, "Come on, Oscar, we got a lot of work to do before it gets dark. Come on!"

In the sixteen years since Oscar had returned to Growing Dreams after earning his degree, the business had grown to almost five million dollars, had nearly seventy employees, and maintained two branch offices. The brothers had nurtured the culture into one that involved everyone in all aspects of the business. They paid tremendous wages and their employees—the best as far as they were concerned—maintained some of the premier properties in the city. Because they'd all learned how to work smarter rather than longer, they had rewarding lifestyles with plenty of time for their families.

"We've come a long way, haven't we, Oscar? It's amazing how the business has evolved. I think back to the decisions we made years ago and how they're still having an impact today. What is it I used to say? 'Our actions and decisions have far-reaching effects.' I didn't know until now how accurate that statement is."

"You didn't use to say that!" Oscar laughed. "I was the one that said it. You were the guy always willing to be happy with just stomping out fires. Remember, 'shoot from the hip' was your philosophy."

"Oh yeah, I guess you're right. So Frank Cutter wants to have dinner with us. What did you tell him?"

"I said absolutely. He offered to buy dinner at Pine Ridge Grille. You know how much I've enjoyed that place over the years. We're meeting him tomorrow night at seven."

"I bet he wants to brag about being acquired by NEW GREEN! This should be interesting. I hope he doesn't stiff us for the check."

The restaurant was as busy as it had been the first night they'd walked into it almost fifteen years ago. That was the night Oscar was introduced to gourmet food and the customer-service formula. Both had been serving him well ever since.

"Good evening, gentlemen!"

"Hello, John," Oscar said, as the two brothers began to search the crowd for Frank Cutter. "John, you've done a tremendous job with this place over the years. I remember when you were just a waiter; now you're the owner."

"Hey, Mr. Cluznik, nobody is just a waiter around here. Nobody is a 'just anything.' Everyone that works here is as important as the next, and of course without them we couldn't ensure that you have an unforgettable dining experience." John was passionate in his words.

"You're always teaching, aren't you, John?" Curtis asked with a smile. "Is a gentleman, and I use the term loosely, by the name of Frank Cutter here yet?"

"Oh yes, sir. Mr. Cutter has been expecting you. Right this way."

It was not exactly a meeting of long lost friends as John brought the two business partners to the table where an aging Frank Cutter was sitting. He quickly ended his telephone conversation and thanked John for bringing his guests to his table. John quickly introduced the waiter for the evening, who hastily went through the menu, took drink orders, and stepped out of the way, sensing the tension at the table. All three tried to make small talk for the next five to ten minutes, skirting the business topics, but each new topic seemed to just fall off the table. Finally, Curtis just blurted it out, a question that undoubtedly had been on his mind.

"Tell me, is Frank Cutter your real name?" Oscar almost bit a hole through his lip to keep from laughing. "I got to know," Curtis continued. "Ever since we caught you trying to steal business in our neighborhood, I've wondered and now I just got to know."

After a short silence, Frank laughed and slapped the table. "No, as a matter of fact, it's not my real name. My real name is Francis, and my dad's name was Francis, and his dad's name was Francis. But Francis Cutter Landscape didn't sound very good to me, so I shortened Francis to Frank."

Now Curtis and Oscar were laughing, knowing that Frank was joking back with them. He'd made a great comeback to Curtis's question. The threesome spent the next two hours enjoying the wonderful steaks and discussing each other's businesses. Frank was very open about his decision to sell his company to the national firm New Green, and when he asked them what they would attribute their success to, the brothers didn't hesitate.

For forty-five minutes Curtis and Oscar talked about the mission statement of Growing Dreams, the fundamental business issues of market, teamwork, training, systems, cost control, and rewards. Most of all, they discussed the success and personal satisfaction they had received by allowing their employees to be active in the decision-making and day-to-day success of the business.

"We help them more by hindering them less," Curtis said proudly. "Our turnover is in the single digits, and because we keep attracting and growing great people, our net profitability is over 17.5%. People wonder what has to be done to be profitable. The answer's simple: keep the same great people coming back year after year."

"That hasn't been my philosophy," Frank said. "My philosophy has always been hands on. That's probably the reason my marriage went south years ago and my employees come and go. Remember Russ? He's on his fourth trip back with us. I need people, so we fire them, he comes back and we hire him again. It goes through the same cycle. And our profit numbers are barely hitting 10%. Yet, New Green liked our business mix and when they made an offer, I was ready to sell. Hey, how about dessert? I bet you like their cherry cheesecake."

"How did you know?" Oscar asked. "We've been eating cherry cheesecake all our lives. This is the second best cheesecake in the world. Curtis and I know a lady here in town that makes the best."

When each had finished off a huge slice of the rich dessert and had drunk several cups of coffee, the conversation seemed to die. For more than three and a half hours these fierce competitors had enjoyed each other's company, but Curtis was starting to feel a little drowsy and was ready to call it a night when Frank Cutter finally got up the courage to pose the question.

"Have you ever thought about selling Growing Dreams, Curtis? I think I could talk with New Green and they would have an interest in acquiring your company. It's a good business and they would take a close look. After all, isn't that what we have ultimately grown our businesses for . . . to sell? What do you think, should I have them call? It's up to you."

Curtis was in a fog and his head was spinning; he couldn't tell if he was awake or asleep. Was he really hearing what he thought he was hearing, or was he dreaming? What would his answer be? He knew he must be dreaming; he couldn't possibly be sitting here with Frank Cutter talking about acquiring businesses and eating cheesecake. But he couldn't be dreaming, because he heard him ask the question again.

"Come on, Curtis, what's it going to be? You give me the answer. It's up to you. What's it going to be?"

Curtis sat up. Hearing the question again, "What's it going to be Curtis? It is up to you. Are you going to sleep on the floor or would you like to try that soft bed you should be in by now? What's it going to be, Son?"

Curtis finally forced his eyes open and saw his dad smiling down at him. He must have fallen asleep and missed the meeting his dad promised they were going to have after dinner. Curtis felt a surge of energy blast through his body. He leaped up from the floor and started trying to tell his dad about the dream he'd just had. "Dad, you wouldn't believe it. Frank Cutter was wanting to acquire our business. Curtis and I had millions of dollars worth of work and Frank Cutter wanted to buy it. WOW! I got to tell Oscar that we need to get a mission statement. That's important. We need to work on one tonight. THEN, we'll get focused on our market, and developing a team. We'll start training programs and define systems. Those are the processes that make a business work good, Dad."

Curtis's dad just picked himself up from the floor where he had flopped during Curtis's enthusiastic dissertation following his insightful sleep. All that he could do was smile and listen as Curtis continued. "Then comes the tough part, Dad. Maybe you can help with this, but everyone in the company has to help with it. That is cost control. Everyone must understand how the company makes money. If they understand, then there are profits . . . and you know what those are, Dad. Profits equal rewards. A company has got to share its rewards. It's all part of the cultural . . . Sorry, Dad, I've got to talk all of this over with OSCAR! Where is Oscar? Dad, we need to stay up a little later. You don't mind, do you, Dad? We're running a business here. It's Friday night. Can we stay up all night? Oscar better not be asleep yet."

Curtis went to the bottom of the stairs and screamed for his brother. Their father decided to use some good advice his dad had shared on rearing children: he would help them more by hindering them less.

"Hey Oscar, come down here. I am fixing me a bologna sandwich. I'll meet you in the kitchen in two minutes. We got to have a meeting about GROWINGGGGG DREAMSSSSSS!

GROWING DREAMS

G<small>ROWING</small> P<small>OINT</small>...

Your actions and decisions have far-reaching effects.

B<small>RAIN</small> P<small>ROBE</small>...

I wonder how many ideas I can develop and put into action that will allow all my dreams to come true?

GROWING DREAMS

Excited **A**bout **L**earning **M**ore **?**

To enhance the great experience of owning your business . . .

Go to www.owners1.com

For other great, inspiring novels by Jim Paluch . . . to find out how to consistently train your people 52 weeks a year . . . or to find out how to experience the energy, storytelling magic and life-changing insights of Jim Paluch in person . . .

Go to www.jphorizons.com

JP Horizons
INCORPORATED